Maritime Memories of PUGET SOUND In Photographs and Text

The only way to go!
Fast transit on Lake Washington
In the good ol' days — steamer Fortuna.

Maritime Memories of PUGET SOUND

In Photographs and Text

By

Joe Williamson and Jim Gibbs

Tacoma, city of destiny, as it appeared in 1878 from an engraving published by the Tacoma Land Company.

Superior PUBLISHING COMPANY

Library of Congress Card Number 76-18150

Library of Congress Cataloging in Publication Data

Gibbs, James Atwood, 1922-
Maritime Memories of Puget Sound.

Includes index.
1. Puget Sound area — History.
I. Williamson, Joe.   II. Title.
F897.P9G52   909'.09'6432   76-18150
ISBN 0-87564-219-5

FIRST EDITION

PRINTED AND BOUND IN CANADA

Harold & Christine Gulbrandsen

CONTENTS

Even to the greatest of navigators and explorers came occasional pitfalls. Here Captain George Vancouver's exploration ship **DISCOVERY** is seen hard on the rocks in Queen Charlotte Sound B.C. Both she and her consort, the **CHATHAM**, seen in the background, went on the reef, but calm waters and the tenacity of the ships' crews managed to work them free without any serious damage, aided by extreme tides. Note the Haida Indians in their canoes examining the situation and hoping to make a prize of the wreck.

About this book

ANYBODY FOR AN ARMCHAIR CRUISE? Just come on aboard and join us as we follow our compass into the yesteryears on Puget Sound. Your crew, "shutterbug" Joe Williamson and "shipwreck" Jim Gibbs, two waterfront characters, friends since the 1940's, who have teamed up in an effort to produce a photo book on a new facet of the maritime past. We have titled it, *Maritime Memories of Puget Sound*, and the title pretty much tells the story. Light on text, with emphasis on thought-provoking maritime photos and captions, it is our hope that a growing number of Puget Sounders will find joy in glimpsing into the past of this very unique corner of Northwest United States. The text for the main part affords a random background of some of the early historic events in Peter Puget land — the Indians, the discoverers, the pioneers, the early settlements, the problems and the establishment of the little ports that grew big and the little ports that faded away. It tells of the beginning of industry and commerce, of the frontiersmen, and the empire builders, the waterfront characters and of those that went from rags to riches and from riches to rags.

The photos that for the most part come from Brer' Joe's vast collection, cover many heretofore unpublished facets and incidents of early Puget Sound. Joe has built his entire career around maritime photography and has also amassed a treasure of photos from valuable collections, many of which have appeared in other books. He has thumbed through some 15,000 negatives to find the ones most appropo for this book, and has his camera — constantly at his side, even when he operates a Seattle sightseeing boat. Many claim Joe has webs between his toes and salt in his veins. His photo shop is in his home at Winslow on the rim of Eagle Harbor and if anything floats on salt-water, fresh-water or stagnant water, he's there to snap it.

Puget Sound ports didn't get off the ground until the California gold rush, when San Francisco cried for timber of every cut. Pioneers who could see beyond gold, found their treasure in green, the tall forests surrounding Puget Sound. They discovered its fabulous fishing waters, coal deposits and productive hinterland valleys. Competition among the lumber mills was something fierce, and coastwise lumber schooners, square-riggers and puffing steamers began to show up to carry the cargo away and bring the passengers and supply for the new frontier around the great inland sea, known as Puget Sound. Occasionally there were Indian flare-ups calling for military action, but the Indian soon learned, to his chagrin, that he must accept the inevitable. Then came the drive for the railroads, a long hard battle of finances and influence as to which port would be the terminus.

The pages of maritime history fade into obscurity amidst the monumental events that have come to pass in our time. The nuclear age is indeed a far cry from the primitive strugglings of slightly over a century ago, but of a certainty, the pioneers must have taken great pride in watching milestones come to pass, sometimes against almost overwhelming odds. With the pressures of our present day, in a computerized and automated world, it is sometimes hard to imagine the exhilarating excitement exhibited by those of yesteryear over such events as the arrival of a ship or the launching of one; the driving of the golden spike as the first train rolled in; a record production of mill timber, or the felling of the largest tree.

It is hoped that the words and photos of this book will revive a small share of the excitement experienced by those stalwarts of yesteryear. Would that we might recapture some of the lost spirit of our forbears who heeded that clarion call, ''Go West, young man! Go West!''

— Jim Gibbs

The Mountain that was God — Mount Rainier, raising its lofty snow-capped dome above the low hanging clouds — filled Vancouver and his men with awe as they explored the waters of Puget Sound. Throughout the decades the fantastic peak, rising more than 14,000 feet, has remained in harmony with the blue waterways of intricate Puget Sound.

Like a forest of masts strung with spiderwebs. These are reflective views of yesteryear at the Port Blakely Mill Co. on Bainbridge Island. At center of upper photo, the **BENJ. F. PACKARD** is flanked by two foreign square-riggers, all of which are taking on lumber with the use of lumber chutes. Lower photo; one feels he is virtually standing on the poop of the four-masted schooner **BLAKELY** which already has most of her deckload stowed aboard. These photos are old Webster & Stevens scenes.

Casting a spell of nostalgia — a bark, a three and two-masted schooner cross courses under a mottled sky, as the sun peeks through to cast a golden path across the dancing waters. The melody is provided by the screeching gulls above.

Like a floating surrey with a fringe on top, the elegant little steamer **MOCK-ING BIRD,** built at Tacoma 1889, accommodates her passengers by bringing them right up to the beach. Note the beau brumel with the stovepipe hat at the oars of the skiff, his lady royally seated in the stern thwart.

Like ghosts out of the past, two formidable square-riggers berth side by side at the old Port Gamble mill to load lumber in olden times. Many such ships took on long timbers through special stern ports.

Introduction

Oh, why should the spirit of mortal be proud?
Like a swift fleeting meteor, a fast flying cloud,
A flash of the lightning, a break of the wave
Man passes from life to his rest in the grave.
—Wm. Knox

Puget Sound! Its very name has a magic ring. As much of a trademark to the Pacific Coast as is Chesapeake Bay to the Atlantic Seaboard, it is America's most unusual inland sea. This great natural body of salt-water often described as a miracle from above has as its guardian saint, lofty Mount Rainier, which raises its dome of eternal white — the mountain that has been called, God. Polka dotted with islands, islets, coves, bays, villages, towns and bustling sea ports, it caters to anything and everything that floats on its surface or lives in its depths. Rich in history, legend and lore, despite our changing times, it has something for just about everyone from the angler to the navigator, or from the yachtsman to the beachcomber. Its waters teem with an endless variety of fish and crustaceans while its fringes are dotted with fascinating beaches of sand or rock, colorful aids to navigation, a wide variety of settlements, and portals of commerce. Sometimes, tall green forests grow within a stone's throw of its beaches.

Travel the world over, but one will never find a comparable body of water; and this is where our story has its beginning, for many discovered its intrigue decades ago, and now it is left to us to reflect on the past with its highlights and pitfalls. The upbuilding of the Sound's shores, from the day of discovery to the present, has been nothing short of phenomenal. Only can we capture through the camera lens those precious moments of yesteryear that otherwise might be lost to memory in this automated age of pressure and hustle.

It was not even 200 years ago that the only human inhabitants on Puget Sound's shores were widely scattered Indian tribes, who, virtually cut off from the outside world lived a relatively peaceful existence in their earthly happy hunting and fishing grounds. Everything was in abundance; they wanted for little. Their numbers were so few, that had not the white man come, the threat of overpopulation, pollution or freeways would have remained forever a never. Nobody knows when the first red man settled on the shores of Puget Sound, but all indications point to the fact that he must have come centuries ago, maybe even anti-dating the birth of Jesus Christ. How they came or where they came from has always been open to speculation. Living a primitive life, they left only a few artifacts to date their coming.

The Puget Sound Indian spent so much time paddling his canoe that his stature was generally short and squat — strong arms and weak legs — unlike his blood brothers dwelling in the hinterlands.

Came the age of exploration as adventurous sea rovers sailed into the hauntingly beautiful waters of Puget Sound. But before delving into this facet of history let us take a glimpse at a statistical description of this great inland sea so as to better understand its personality, as did the early explorers. Puget Sound is considered a bay with numerous channels and branches, extending about 90 miles southward from the Strait of Juan de Fuca to Olympia, most southerly port and the capital of Washington State. The northern boundary is formed, at its main entrance, by a line between Point Wilson on the Olympic Peninsula and Point Partridge on Whidbey Island, (second largest island in continental United States) Deception Island, and Sares Head on Fidalgo Island; and at a third entrance at the south end of Swinomish Channel between Fidalgo Island and McGlinn Island. There are places within this great body of water where the depths exceed 900 feet, and generally speaking, the hazards are few because of the deep waters. Navigation is comparatively easy in clear weather, and the main channels are well marked by navigation aids. Generally a mid-channel course can be followed without fear of stranding. The currents follow the general direction of the channels and have considerable velocity. In thick or dirty weather, owing to the uncertainty of the currents, the great depths render soundings useless in many places. Such facts are well known to the pilots and navigators of our day, but not so in the age of discovery when each bay, cove and inlet had to be approached with caution and sounded with the lead line.

Actually, Puget Sound has grown with the years. The name when first applied took in only about half of the area it does today. In fact, the northern part of what we call Puget Sound is officially known as Admiralty Inlet, while the lower part is Puget Sound. Further, the title ''Puget Sound country,'' reaches all the way north to the San Juan Islands bordering British Columbia, the 172 island archipelago often described, along with Ireland, as a ''little bit of Heaven that fell from out the sky one day.'' Perhaps the great extension of the name Puget stems from the fact that the largest and most prosperous port cities are located in that section originally designated as Puget Sound from the time of Captain George Vancouver's discovery. The highly honored lieutenant of the great navigator's ship, Peter Puget, would have been greatly elated to know that it is his name above all others that has been preserved in the pages of history. His commander attached it to the waterway, in May of 1792.

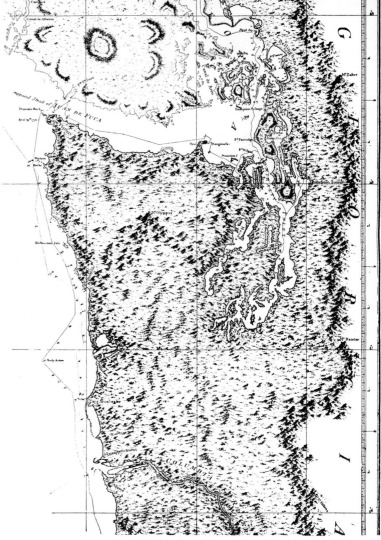

A section of the chart of the elite Captain George Vancouver, R.N., discoverer of Puget Sound. It shows the names bestowed by him and other early explorers, along the Washington Coast, the Strait of Juan de Fuca, Admiralty Inlet and Puget Sound. It further shows that Admiralty Inlet, not Puget Sound, was the major body of water originally. The Puget Sound area is denoted at the southern end of the waterway only. It further shows that part of the island of Quadra and Vancouver would now belong to the United States had the 49th parallel, throughout its whole length to the Pacific, been insisted upon in 1846, as it had been in all previous negotiations.

Those curious poles at Port Discovery were the object of speculation by Captain Vancouver's men. It was later learned that the Indians used them to support nets by which they caught wild ducks and geese when approaching or leaving the water.

Chapter One
Indian Ways and Discovery Days

*Those old stories of visions and dreams
guiding men have their truth; we are
saved by making the future present
to ourselves.*

—George Eliot

CAPTAIN GEORGE VANCOUVER, ranks along with Captain James Cook as one of the world's greatest early navigators and explorers. His vivid descriptions, daring exploits and accurate charting, along with his diplomacy have endeared him forever in the annals of history. He entered the navy at the age of 13 and served three years as a boy under Captain Cook aboard the *Resolution*, advancing quickly through the ranks to one of Britain's most able seafarers. It was he, in the spring of 1792, that dispatched his second lieutenant, Peter Puget of the flagship *Discovery,* to explore what we know today as Puget Sound.

Peter Puget who sailed around the world with Vancouver and went on to a distinguished naval career, joined shipmaster Joseph Whidbey (for whom Whidbey Island was named) in the ship's boats from the *Discovery* and *Chatham* to initially explore the waters of the Sound. They were followed by Lieutenant Joseph Baker (for whom Mt. Baker was named) in the ship's yawl, each craft branching out into different areas of the great inland sea. On their return, it was noted in the vessel's journal:

"Thus by our joint efforts we had completely explored every turning of this extensive inlet; and to commemorate Mr. Puget's exertions, the south extremity of it, I (George Vancouver) named Puget's Sound."

Though other brave Spanish, British, French, Yankee and Russian explorers made celebrated discoveries along the North Pacific rim, it was left for Vancouver to make a thorough survey of Puget Sound which was so reliable and accurate that his findings were used for decades afterwards. In a way of speaking, he actually opened Puget Sound to the world at large. Though disappointed at not finding the fabled Northwest Passage, neither through the Strait of Juan de Fuca or Puget Sound, these two great bodies of water were to become the maritime highway of commerce for both Northwest America and for Western Canada.

As earlier mentioned, when the explorers initially came to Puget Sound, the only sign of habitation they found was an occasional Indian village tucked behind a sandspit or in some deep cove. As in other sections of what is now the United States, the native's greatest foe was the steady, uncontrolled advance of the white man, who by taking unfair advantage eventually crowded him off of his coveted land. Occasionally there would be an uprising — but with few exceptions the outcome was always the same — defeat. Tainted promises and banishment to restricted reservations was all the Indian received from the treaties.

The age old life style of the Indian was repulsive to the invader and with few exceptions his rights were infringed upon with little feeling or remorse, and yet despite it all, many a Puget Sound native befriended the white man and in frequent cases warned him of planned attacks by hostiles of their own Indian bloodline.

Thousands of Northwest Indians succumbed to white man's diseases, previously unknown to them. Also introduced was "firewater," which was consumed by the ignorant savages with great relish, turning many into disreputable alcoholics, they having no knowledge of how to control its usage. Venereal disease spread rapidly, and when the Indians were shoved onto reservations, most lost their will and purpose for life. Only the missionary and Indian agents showed compassion and even they found opposition in taking the side of the tribes in the face of adversity.

Before being banished, the summer residences of the coastal Indians were temporary lodges built of rushes or bark, but their winter abodes to protect from the dank, rainy, cold days were more permanent. Cedar planks or driftwood, two or three feet wide and from three to six inches thick, were cut with crude wedges made of elk horn or with chisels of beaver teeth and flint. From such planks and from big logs were fashioned rectangular houses, 50 to 100 feet in length and 15 to 20 feet in width. Openings were left along the ridgepole in the roof to permit smoke to escape, and a singular door was provided for entry or departure. Such "long houses" provided for a number of families living in one massive room, lined with bunks. Fire pits, one for each family, were the center of activities. The floor was merely the earth on which the house stood.

Main food staples consisted of salmon, caught in their age-old traps or weirs; halibut, cod and sturgeon were also prized. Shellfish such as clams, muscles and oysters were eaten with great relish, and ancient Indian encampment sites could often be located by the great piles of shells which remained long after the Indian houses had fallen into rot and dust. Other favorite seafood sought by the Northwest Indians from fresh water lakes and streams were trout and bass. The forests abounded with elk, deer and bear and the natives were never without an abundance of fresh meat. To balance their diet they collected herbs, berries, nuts, roots and bulbs.

The Puget Sound Indians lived a good life, although their intelligence and initiative were limited to their own little world, until the coming of the white man. When vermin made their abodes no longer habitable they would merely move to another location.

During the mild seasons the men wore a robe or blanket thrown over their backs and fastened across the chest by a cord, or went about stark naked, although the higher chiefly class and shamans (the latter, sort of a medicine man who dispersed evil spirits) possessed woven hats, moccasins, leggings, breechcloths, buckskin shirts, etc., while the women dressed in a frock of twisted strings of cedar bark or grass, fastened to a cord or band around the waist, falling to the knees. The boast of the men were their dugout cedar canoes and wood carvings, and of the women, crude weaving of dog hair, shredded bark or coverings made from bear skins. They also did basketry, using cedar bark and dried rushes.

Be it ever so humble, there's no place like home. Built of boards split from cedar logs, this print shows the inside of a Northwest Indian longhouse in which several families would live, mostly during the inclement months. Some of the longhouses were 100 feet long.

Social classes existed among the coastal bands, although there was neither a totemic nor a clan system like that developed among the peoples of the northland. Society was divided into a hereditary nobility, a middle class, and a slave class composed mainly of captives taken in war, along with their descendents. The tribal chief had the final say in all matters, and marriages between nobility and commoners were frowned upon. There was no womens' liberation, the female being given the drudgery of the daily chores. In many ways, their government was akin to that of early Hawaii, and beliefs existed strongly in personal guardian spirits in their religious life. In many controversial problems, tribal councils met around a fire for discussions, always relying on the opinion of their chiefs.

Feuds or battles were not uncommon among rival tribes, though some were much more peaceful than others. There was plenty of everything for everyone and generally little reason for fighting. But fight they did, a trademark of man almost from the beginning of time. Perhaps the greatest foe of the Puget Sound and Strait Indians were the warlike Haidas who paddled their great canoes down from the northern shores of British Columbia. Pitched battles were fought on the beaches and often the raiding parties, like the Norsemen, would retreat with a load of spoils and a host of captives which became their slaves.

A hallmark of the Puget Sound Indian was the potlatch, a ceremonial feast at which gifts were distributed to friends and neighboring tribesmen, each of whom was to in turn respond in like manner at a potlatch of his own.

Today, only crumbs of what used to be exist, central agencies in the state administering over Indian reservations such as the Taholah Indian Agency with jurisdiction over the Quinault, Makah, Squaxin Island, Nisqually, Skokomish, Chehalis and Ozette reservations, while the Tulalip Agency is concerned with the Tulalip, Puyallup, Swinomish, Lummi, Port Madison and Muckleshoot tribes.

With a better understanding of the Northwest Indian, let us again return to the age of exploration and of the events leading up to Vancouver's discovery of Puget Sound.

For nearly three centuries maritime powers of Europe had searched for the elusive Strait of Anian, better known as the Northwest Passage, which was to have linked the Atlantic with the Pacific. Imperial Spain was first to get its foot in the door. In 1542, Bartolome Ferrelo, commanding a Spanish expedition, sailed northward along the California coast searching for the passage. He terminated his search without success, on the southern Oregon coast.

In 1579, came Sir Francis Drake, who sailed up the Northwest coast and named the land, New Albion. He sailed as far north as the 48th parallel, becoming the first

First house in Jefferson County, built at Port Townsend by A. A. Plummer in 1851. For a time it served as the home of all the earliest settlers of Port Townsend.

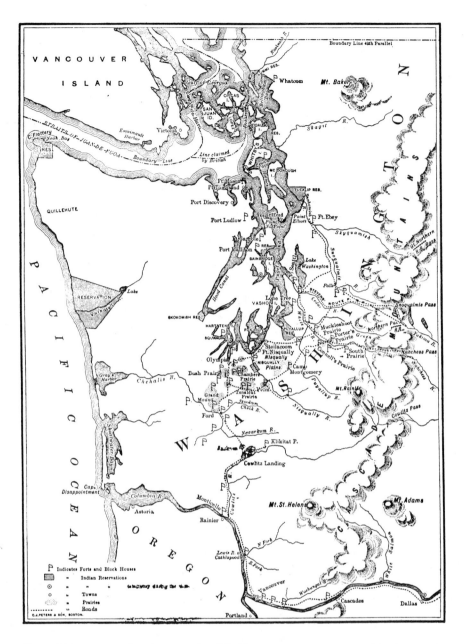

An early map of Western Washington territory, showing the sites of early Indian battlegrounds and reservations, plus roads, towns and other features during the pioneer era.

Caucasian to see what is now the Washington coast, and that was 41 years before the pilgrims landed at Plymouth Rock.

Then, in 1592, came the legendary Juan de Fuca, who allegedly sailed under Spanish colors. A Greek pilot, with the given name of Apostolos Valerianos, he told of entering a broad inlet between the 47th and 48th degrees of north latitude. His story was later published in the book, *Purchas, His Pilgrimes,* in 1625, and his account was generally accepted by most explorers thereafter. For the most part, it was the latter day historians who labeled him a colossal liar. de Fuca discovered the Strait of Juan de Fuca, which today bears his name, but did not proceed to the end of the Striat or into the waters of what are known today as Puget Sound.

Northwest history then lapses into a void. Finally in 1670, Charles II of England granted a charter to "The Company of Adventurers of England Trading into Hudson's Bay," whose sole purpose was to discover a new passage into the South Seas, and to find a source of trade. The crown granted the company a monopoly.

Then Russia got into the picture endeavoring to become the primacy of the Pacific. Peter the Great, boldly announced to his subjects that the mother country would take over all territory in North America not already occupied by other powers. To Vitus Bering, a Dane, fell the role of discovery. On receiving the blessings of Catherine, successor to Peter, he set out on two expeditions in the North Pacific under the most undesirable of conditions, discovering the inter-continental strait that today carries his name, charting out the grim Aleutian archipelago and the Alaska mainland. When he succumbed in 1741, he still firmly believed that Alaska was an island separated from the mainland by the fabled Northwest Passage. Russia established its first permanent settlement in Alaska in 1784 and hung on without any substantial progress until 1867, when Uncle Sam took the great northland off its hands for a mere $7.2 million. It was another of Russia's ill-starred ventures in gaining control in the Pacific — previously bowing out in California, the Pacific Northwest and Hawaii.

France was never a real threat to dominance of the Pacific Northwest, being pretty much eliminated from aggression by the Treaty of Paris in 1763, which set up a continuing showdown battle between England and Spain. The latter power flexed its muscle and initially appeared to have the upper hand, sending expeditions along the Northwest coast and later into the Strait of Juan de Fuca. Juan Perez sighted a mountain which he named Santa Rosalia (Mt. Olympus), highest of the Olympic range, and Bruno Heceta and Juan de la Bodega made a beachhead at Point Grenville in 1775, in the name of Spain. It was Heceta again that was credited with sighting the locale of the Columbia River entrance, which he called, ''River of the West,'' but into which he failed to enter or even make an attempt to do so.

Next came the indomitable Captain James Cook, generally described as the greatest navigator, and explorer ever to come out of England. He had orders to lay claim to any unoccupied lands in the Northwest. Sighting land off Oregon's central coast, he then proceeded to Nootka, on Vancouver Island, where he made an anchorage and remained for a month. Making a careful survey of the coastline north of the entrance to the Strait of Juan de Fuca, the broad strait somehow eluded him.

In 1785, La Perouse sailed up the Northwest Coast in the *LaBoussole* and *Astrolabe,* penetrating well into Alaska, leaving behind a detailed account of his three year Pacific voyage.

In 1787, young Captain Charles William Barkley, sailing in the *Imperial Eagle* on a fur trading expedition, found and named the Strait of Juan de Fuca which had escaped the view of all other navigators after Juan de Fuca. Barkley, an Englishman, sailing under Austrian colors to evade procuring a license from the East India Company, shared the news of his good fortune with John Meares, a former lieutenant in the British Navy, who was planning a trading voyage to the Northwest Coast. He and another English explorer, William Douglas, flying both the Portugese flag and the Union Jack, joined forces in their endeavor which was to place a new dimension on Northwest trading. In 1788, the two mariners established

The Seattle waterfront in olden times witnessed a generous share of Indians come to its shores. Who had a better right? For was it not the Indians who were the rightful owners of the shores of Puget Sound? Here a large group of Siwash Indians camp along the beach of what is today known as the foot of Bell Street. They sold their catches of salmon and other goods to the settlers. This photo was taken in 1883.

a real foothold at Nootka by purchasing a parcel of land from a native chief, so as to make it all legal and official.

From then on everybody got into the act. John Kendrick and Robert Gray, financed by a Boston syndicate, arrived in the *Columbia Redivivia* and *Washington* that same year, bent on filling their ships' holds with furs for which the markets of the world were ripe. At about the same time, Spain bristled against England by sending Estevan Jose Martinez to Nootka Sound in 1789. He headed a naval force which claimed the island for Spain, seizing several English vessels. Meares, however, escaped and put on full sail for England carrying the distressing news to the crown in London. Though the monarchy's hackles were raised, Spain meant business, and to fortify its claim sent a second naval force to the Northwest in 1790 under Francisco Eliza to occupy and fortify the Nootka area and to possess the entrance to the Strait of Juan de Fuca by virtue of a small brick fortification which his men built at Neah Bay, a structure which completely baffled the Makah Indians.

Manuel Quimper, Eliza's lieutenant, was then ordered to the eastern end of the Strait of Juan de Fuca where he turned northward to explore the San Juan Islands and to sight what we know today as Mount Baker. Unfortunately he terminated his exploration voyage before entering Admiralty Inlet, narrowly missing the discovery of that inlet and of Puget Sound.

As war clouds between England and Spain hung on the horizon, a parley was held at Nootka, the two powers signing a "convention" allowing for the appointment of commissioners, one for each nation, who were to dispose of the problem at issue. Nobody bothered to invite the Indians. They didn't even get a chance to pass around the peace pipe. Captain George Vancouver represented England and Juan Francisco de la Bodega y Quadra was the voice of authority for Spain, both men being of good judgement. They were able to resolve their differences through arbitration, thus preventing another war. The "convention" was signed on February 12, 1793, whereby both powers agreed to abandon Nootka Sound, and whereby Spain agreed to make restitution for property seized. Still nobody would smoke the Indians' peace pipe.

Prior to the signing, Vancouver had been at work discovering and exploring Puget Sound. Proudly telling of his new discovery, the explorer was virtually enthralled with what his eyes beheld.

"Nothing," said he, "can be more striking than the beauty of these waters without a shoal or a rock or any danger whatever for the whole length of this internal navigation, the finest in the world."

He praised the great beauty of the waterway and then added, "I venture nothing in saying that there is no country in the world that possesses waters equal to these."

Wow! Could they have used this guy in the Chamber of Commerce!

This is the way it used to be — the main line of traffic on Puget Sound — by Indian dugout canoe, and those two "genuine" squaws are paddling to a white settlement to trade their goods, way, way back when.

Vancouver's mission was two fold; first, as a representative of the English government, he was to proceed to Nootka, where he was to receive from the Spanish authorities, "the buildings, districts or parcels of land, which were occupied by the subjects of His Britannic Majesty in April 1789, and, second, to make an accurate survey of the coast, from the 35th degree of north latitude, northward to the 60th parallel; to ascertain particularly the number, situation and extent of the settlements of civilized nations within these limits; and especially to acquire information as to the nature and direction of any water passage, which might serve as a channel, for commercial intercourse between that side of America and the territories on the Atlantic side occupied by British subjects."

Let us again take up the voyage of the HMS *Discovery* and her consort *Chatham* sailing through the Strait of Juan de Fuca. We find them near New Dungeness, where all hands were engaged in conversation about a number of tall, straight poles erected perpendicularly along the shore. Because the Indians at the nearby encampment could not speak the language of the more northerly Nootkan tribes with which some of the crew were familiar, they were unable to learn the reasons for the poles. Each was supported by spurs or braces, so as to fix them in an upright position. At first they were believed for use in drying fish or for religious, civil or military purposes. It was later learned that these poles were for catching waterfowl in marshy areas, as they took off in flight. Nets

spread between the poles (75 to 100 feet high) ensnared the birds and allowed the Indians to capture them as an additive to their diet. Thus it was that Captain Vancouver's men became acquainted with the new ways of the natives that inhabited the shores near the entrance to Admiralty Inlet and Puget Sound.

Vancouver's flagship, the *Discovery,* was a sizeable vessel of about 400 tons, while the *Chatham,* was less than half her size. As these two vessels lay at anchor in Port Discovery Bay, the cutter, longboat and pinnace were dispatched to continue the exploration. On the morning of May 7, 1792 they skirted Protection Island eastward through a penetrating fog. After moving along in a silent sea for about eight miles, a sandy point was rounded to which was given the name Wilson, in honor of Vancouver's good friend, Captain George Wilson of the British Navy. The local Indians called it "Kam Kam ho," but brother Wilson won out and the point bears his name to this day. It continues as the principal turning point for ships entering Admiralty Inlet from the Strait of Juan de Fuca. Since 1879, the point has been marked by a lighthouse.

The fog hung low as the little armada moved on, rounding and naming Point Hudson. Suddenly, as if a fairy had raised the magic wand, the clammy veil of fog evaporated; before them loomed an incomparable beauty. To the northeast, a lofty snow-capped mountain rose above the green foothills. It was Mount Baker, named a few days

In time, the Indians had adopted white man's dress but still busied themselves with goods to barter, such as in this early scene taken in the harbor at Everett.

The Indian dugout canoe, long the basic mode of water travel on Puget Sound, centuries before the white man came. Here, some charming belles of yesteryear, borrow one from an Indian friend for a Sunday outing on Puget Sound.

earlier for 3rd Lieutenant Joseph Baker, one of 100 officers and enlisted men aboard the *Discovery.* The *Chatham* carried 45. Against the western horizon, the sawtooth peaks of the Olympics touched the blue sky. Most striking of all, however, in full majesty at the southerly end of the great inland sea — 14,000 feet high was a mountain breathtaking to behold. To this peak with its eternal snows, the explorer attached the name, Rainier, to honor Rear Admiral Rainier of the British Navy. Many decades later, Tacomans tried to change it to Mt. Tacoma or Tahoma, but the old admiral who had long since been laid to his rest, continued to rest in peace, for the handle Vancouver attached to the peak was to remain.

Vancouver, who had a flare for writing, described the scenes in words that have never been equalled by the most prolific of writers. With excitement, his men entered the commodious harbor to which the name Townshend (Townsend) was applied after the marquis of the same signature. On exploring the harbor, the party landed on a high, steep cliff on which Vancouver observed an unusual deposit of ''undurated clay, much resembling fuller's earth,'' which upon closer examination he found to be ''a rich species of marrow stone'' and therefore named it Marrowstone Point.

Continuing onward, the boats fanned out to the bays and inlets, the officers doing such a magnificent job of charting and surveying, that their findings became a bible for navigators. Vancouver had learned his lessons well from Captain Cook ''that once a coast has been discovered one is derelict in his duty if failing to chart it with accuracy.''

During the following weeks, Whidbey, Bainbridge, Vashon and a host of other islands and geographical features were charted. One party rounded Foulweather Bluff, and navigated narrow and tantalizing Hood Canal (named for Admiral Viscount Hood). One boat also moved as far south as Dash Point, near the present site of Tacoma.

It was nearing the end of June, and after exploring and naming Bellingham Bay and Birch Bay, the *Discovery* and *Chatham*, which had followed the smaller craft into Puget Sound, now proceeded northward, through the Gulf, the Strait of Georgia and Johnstone Strait to Queen Charlotte Sound to find more new and startling discoveries. But, nothing Vancouver found on his further exploration was to prove more exciting and promising than Puget Sound.

End of an era — Indians sell basketry work on Seattle's downtown streets in the 1920's. Such scenes are relegated to the past as the art is seldom practiced on the reservations anymore.

This vine-covered log cabin was supposedly the first house in Port Townsend, dating back to the middle of the last century. The "dear heart" at the entrance looks like a person anyone would be proud to call their grandma. Redding's Studio photo.

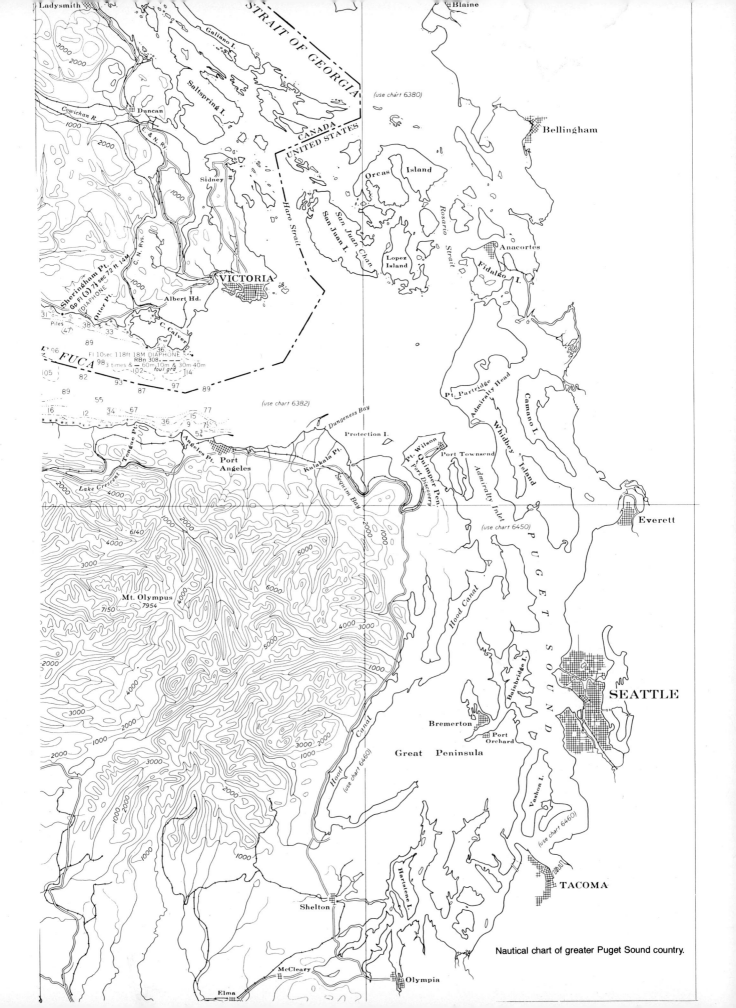

Nautical chart of greater Puget Sound country.

The old blockhouse at Coupeville dating from the mid 1850's, as it appeared in 1929. The structure remains as a shrine to the glorious past, one of the prime attractions on Whidbey Island.

Three old photos pieced together to give a wide-angle view of historic Port Madison in the year 1880. These are among the oldest known photos of the long defunct port mill town, which once was one of the largest lumber exporters on the Sound. The ships, at right, are the square-riggers **TIDAL WAVE, OAKLAND, VIDETTE,** and somewhere, not visible, the hulk of the wrecked **FREE TRADE,** towed into the port after being abandoned off Quillayute Rocks in 1878.

The building and the launching of a commercial wooden sailing schooner. The year was 1897, and the schooner, the **ANNIE M. CAMPBELL.** The place was the Hall Bros. shipyard at Port Blakely. The man in the white beard, fifth from the left, (upper photo) is believed to be James Hall, potentate of the historic yard.

A stately study in canvas. The schooner **ANNIE CAMPBELL**, built by the Hall yard, roamed the Pacific most of her career, hauling lumber, copra and coal. For several years she was owned by Captain J.E. Shields. Her end came in 1926 when wrecked in the Marquesas.

One of the earliest known photos of Port Gamble's Puget Mill Company (Pope & Talbot). The faded photo gives a panoramic view of the entire mill with a host of square-riggers and fore n' afters taking on lumber for world ports.

Chapter Two
Portal to Commerce

*Commerce defies every wind, outrides
every tempest, and invades every zone.*
— Bancroft

RAPID CHANGES IN THE modes and methods of water transportation on Puget Sound in recent years would have made our forbears scratch their heads in bewilderment. Before Vancouver's arrival and for a few decades thereafter, only by primitive dugout or canoe did the Indian ford the waterways. If these were not available he stripped and leaped into the icy brine, but not for long. It was, and still is, mighty cold.

When the settlers came, a new era opened, though for many years the windship was the ultimate in water transportation, while on land man traveled by horseback, muleback, wagon or oxcart. If none of these conveyances were at hand, the two feet that God gave him performed adequately. As time marched on, the era of the inland sea steamer and the stagecoach gave a whole new dimension to the life style of the pioneers, but it was many years, in fact, right up through the turn of the century before the commercial sailing vessel was pushed aside by the "smoke puffers."

To the California goldrush the Pacific Northwest owed its incentive to grow. Demands in the golden state called for a mixture of green — green to the tune of the tall-timbered shores of Puget Sound. After 1849, big things began to happen. Small towns popped up like mushrooms around little sawmills, where saws buzzed with increasing frequency. There was a pressing need in San Francisco for lumber and piling; Puget Sound had it and could supply. The only way to transport the timber was by sailing ship, and under acres of canvas and a variety of flags they arrived, not only loading for the trip to the Golden Gate but for sectors throughout the world. The word was out about those tall fir trees.

Shipyards were erected next to the mills, for it was much less expensive to build wooden ships on the spot than to export lumber elsewhere for a similar purpose. It was a colorful era as places like Port Gamble, Port Ludlow, Port Blakely, Utsalady, Port Orchard, Seabeck or Port Madison, to name a few, began to make news. Port Townsend, so strategically located, was visioned as the chief port for the entire Puget Sound area, and was headed in that direction until embryo villages such as Seattle, Tacoma, Steilacoom and Olympia began seeking rail connections with the nation outside. For many years Port Townsend's harbor was a forest of masts and its little Barbary coast was second only to that of San Francisco. Rough, tough characters haunted the saloons; crimps runners, pimps, prostitutes played upon the weakness of the flesh in sailors weary from long months at sea. "Gin mills" and "mad houses" provided the "recreation," which lasted till one's money gave out. Then were adminstered the knockout drops, and "jack" would find himself reviving on the deck of a rolling ship from the application of a bucket of cold salt water. Only then would he realize that he had been shanghaied, having been deposited through a trapdoor in some waterfront dive while still prostrate. Blood money was handed over in accordance with the size and potential of the "prey," or the urgency of the vessel skipper, who often turned out to be a tyrant.

Amid the growing fleets of sailing vessels — schooners, brigs, brigantines, barks, barkentines and full-rigged ships, the steamer made its appearance. One exception to the fact was the Hudson's Bay Company steamer *Beaver* which actually traveled on the waters of Puget Sound many years before any others of her breed made an appearance. Well before her time, she came west under the British flag all the way from England in 1835-36, making her home at Victoria, B.C., under Hudson's Bay Co. For five decades her sidewheels were to stir up Northwest waters.

Not until 1853 did the first American steamer appear in local waters. Little to brag about, she was a squat, pint-sized sidewheeler with the name *Fairy,* but her wand must have stuck for she had a notorious ability for being cranky and disgustingly behind schedule. Joined the following year by a counterpart, the *Major Tompkins,* the Sound village folk were sure they would now be better accommodated. A contract for a weekly mail service was granted to the steamer, but alas, the good *Major* blew it in the winter of 1855 when a winter storm deposited her on the outcroppings of lower Vancouver Island, a position from which she did not recover.

At that very moment, Puget Sound was suffering birth pangs. Before long, demands brought more formidable steamboats like the *Eliza Anderson*, which puffed into Peter Puget's pond after completion at Portland, Oregon in 1859. Ahead of her were four decades of valuable service.

Settlements came to life along the Duwamish and Snohomish rivers and river sternwheelers with shallow-drafts were roughed out to meet the demands — the *Clara Brown, Comet, Wenat* and *Black Diamond* to name but a few. They carried anything and everything for a fee. It wasn't unusual to see a squealing pig running rough shod over a snoozing passenger, or a rooster trying to outcrow the steamer's whistle. Stopping at anything that even resembled a landing, and often just running up on the river bank for a load of cord wood to keep the boilers hot, these pioneer steamboats and their devil-may-care operators and "navigators" somehow got the job done.

An old Indian trail was improved to provide a stagecoach route between the Columbia River and Olympia, and this in turn gave added incentive, not only to Olympia but also to Steilacoom, Shelton and Tacoma, all vying for prominent positions in fierce competition at the southerly end of Puget Sound.

On completion of the Union-Central Pacific Railroad to California in 1863, empire builders cast an eye to an extension to the Pacific Northwest.

By 1870, steamboating had reached large proportions. The Oregon Steam Navigation Company operating on the Columbia River was expanding, and the vast wealth of both the river and of Puget Sound was beginning to be realized. Though inter-continental rail line connections

Elisha P. Ferry, first governor of the State of Washington. A native of Monroe, Michigan, born August 9, 1825, he was admitted to the bar in 1845 and in 1869, was appointed surveyor-general of Washington. He was governor of the territory from 1872 to 1880, and after practicing law in Seattle from 1880-1887 became vice president of the Puget Sound National Bank. Ferry was elected governor of the State, October 1, 1889.

Colonel Michael T. Simmons, the first American settler to explore the country north of the Columbia River, and the first to make a home on Puget Sound. He later built the initial sawmill and gristmill on Puget Sound. One of the purchasers of the brig **ORBIT**, the first ship owned by residents of the territory, this Olympia merchant was a leader in every public enterprise.

with water transportation were still a way off, a Kalama to Tacoma rail link was completed in 1873 bringing the river and the Sound in close touch. At almost the same time, 1872-75 the "Rawhide line" a narrow gauge railroad between Walla Walla and Wallula went into operation giving an advantage to the Columbia River, while the planned Seattle-Walla Walla rail line ran into bankruptcy after only 20 miles of track had been laid down. Meanwhile both Northern Pacific and later, Great Northern worked their way gradually west, with an eye toward trans-continent reality, but this facet we shall cover later in our little episode.

While the rails were punching it out, there was even keener rivalry in the 1880's between steamship operators on Puget Sound. Rate wars were frequent, and dog-eat-dog competition broke out on most routes. The independent operators found rough sledding against the heavily financed organizations, and many fell by the wayside.

In deepsea operations, the first regular steamship service between Puget Sound and San Francisco was begun on a monthly basis as early as 1867, and by 1886, Puget Sound had become the gateway to Alaska offering regular passenger, freight and mail service. Doing the initial honors was the venerable SS *Ancon,* which gained the press by returning from the northland, with among other cargo, some $35,000 in gold.

In 1891, Northern Pacific Railroad placed the SS *Phra*

Nang in service from Tacoma to the Orient, much to the chagrin of Seattleites. The latter city got back in 1895 with the establishment of the Alaska Steamship Company, and a year later, when the Japanese steamship *Miike Maru* became the first transpacific liner to link Puget Sound directly with Japan.

Then came the greatest shot in the arm of all — the Klondike gold discovery of 1897-98. Virtually overnight, the struggling little town of Seattle became a beehive of activity. Men and ships of every description began arriving just as they had done at San Francisco in 1849. From every direction of the compass did they come and the excitement rose to a fever pitch. Nothing so stirs man as does the thought of his pockets bulging with gold nuggets. Gold was on everyone's mind and individuals were willing to pay any price or take any kind of berth to get to Alaska. When the SS *Portland,* pulled into port with a ton of gold, a zealous news reporter got it in bold headlines, and the town went mad, despite the fact that another ship had arrived just a few days earlier with more than a ton of gold, but without the publicity. Seattle no longer was a struggling lumber port but a thriving commercial and supply center for "operation gold fever."

Only after 1889 did Washington cease being a territory and become a state, but never had it witnessed anything like this. Every conveyance that would float went north, loaded to the gunwhales with men and cargo.

Venerable steamer **BEAVER**, first steam powered vessel to operate on the North Pacific, and second to cross the Atlantic. She was built at Blackwall, England, in 1834-35, coming around the Horn to the Columbia River, via Honolulu, under sail. After her paddlewheels were attached, she cruised Puget Sound and British Columbia waters, and as far north as Russian Alaska in the service of the Hudson's Bay Company. Sold to a logging firm in 1874, she served as a towing craft until going on the rocks at the entrance to Vancouver B.C. harbor in 1888.

First protestant church north of the Columbia River, was this pioneer church at Steilacoom, brought about by the efforts of the Reverend John F. Devore, who with the aid of pioneers constructed it in 1854.

Old Olympia at the south end of Puget Sound, played a big role in the early maritime history of the area, and almost from the beginning was destined to become the capital city of Washington State. This is the way the rough and rugged port town appeared, probably about 1862. How times have changed.

Pioneer spiritual leader, Methodist minister Reverend John F. Devore, native Kentuckian, born in 1817, came to Oregon in 1853 and built the church at Steilacoom, first in the territory, north of the Columbia and later another church at Olympia. He died in Tacoma in 1888.

Old Fort Nisqually, a small fort of the Hudson's Bay Company, and later of the Puget Sound Agricultural Company, was established on the shore of the Sound, near the mouth of the Nisqually River, in 1833, and was famous in the pioneer period after the American settlers came to the territory. It was established with the expectation of making it the center of colonizing the Puget Sound Country, with a hold placed on it by the British. It was the center of activities during the Indian uprisings, but in later years passed from the scene, though since restored as a shrine.

Many of the unseaworthy craft never reached Juneau, Skagway or Nome. Some even broke down before reaching British Columbia waters or left their carcasses draped over some outcrop along the Inside Passage. But the armada to Alaska continued. New ship lines were formed but only a handful still maintained regular service after the turn of the century.

With the opening of the Panama Canal in 1914, Puget Sound had a prosperous new water link that put it weeks closer to the Eastern Seaboard and to Gulf ports, a far cry from the strain of rounding Cape Horn at the bitter end of South America.

As San Francisco opened her Golden Gate, the gates of Puget Sound likewise opened wide, its ports catering to deepsea vessels in the coasting and foreign trades — all flags, all breeds. Further, this great body of water became a mecca for naval vessels with a giant repair yard at Bremerton; it quickly became known as the finest cruising area for pleasure craft in the entire United States and the home of sizable tug and barge operations and commercial fishing fleets. Peter Puget's waterways were without precedent, and the uniqueness was added to in 1916 with the opening of the Lake Washington Ship Canal, which through the use of locks permitted deepwater ships to gain entrance to two fresh water lakes — Union and Washington — and shallow-draft small craft could go it one better by traversing a slough to lake Sammamish.

On into the age of atoms, containers and automation, Puget Sound became inhabited by millions of people, a far cry from the day when Peter Puget saw it for the first time. But despite its tremendous growth in a relatively few decades, it remains in much part a beautiful body of water, preserving many tantalizing haunts. On a clear spring day, when coming by vessel into the Sound one cannot help but sharing somewhat the same thrill experienced by Captain Vancouver and his men.

Perhaps it is best summed up by the pen of John Whittier:

I hear the tread of pioneers —
 The millions yet to be;
The first low wash of waves where soon
 Shall roll a human sea.

The dreams and visions of the early pioneers and empire builders were to become reality and then some. They called it progress. Today in our fast moving environment we must pause for a moment to reflect on the way it used to be and then ask ourselves: Was it worth it? The golden memories of yesteryear grow more fragile and are soon relegated to well worn history books and faded photographs. Not many among us would really want to go back, but we who are enthralled by the maritime world of today and yesterday appreciate the memories, fully realizing that like vapor they quickly fade into nothingness with each succeeding generation.

One of the little Puget Sound seafront towns that never quite got off the ground is Eglon, on the North Kitsap Peninsula. A very old photo of the funny little village is seen here. Note the womens' dress.

One of the many pioneer waterfront towns that didn't quite make it. Lowell, near Everett as it appeared in 1887, never came to full bloom.

This is as far as the pioneer shallow-draft river boats could go — Fall City on the Snoqualmie River, below the falls that drop over a great chasm. This town was once known as, The Landing, and its history goes back to the 1880's. It is still a pastoral town in our day.

Those good old days of river steamboatin' come back to life in this nostalgic scene on the Snohomish waterfront in the early 1890's. From left, the steamers **W. K. MERWIN** and the **MAY QUEEN.** Early in 1896, the **MERWIN,** commanded by the skipper of the same name, collided with the half-open railroad drawspan at Mount Vernon on the Skagit. The steamer came out second best, losing her stack, pilot house and texas. Captain Merwin darted from the pilothouse in the nick of time and came out with only a few injuries. The **MAY QUEEN,** an 86 ton craft, built at Seattle in 1886, and registered at Port Townsend, was once owned by pioneer maritime personality Captain George Gove. In the lower photo, the river port of Snohomish (on the Snohomish River) is seen as it appeared in 1887.

Three sternwheelers crowd into the Olympia docks from various Sound points, well before the turn of the century. From right, they are the **MULTNOMAH, GREYHOUND** and another not identified. In the foreground is the tug **SANDMAN**. Pictured in the lower photo, the harbor is even busier, with four sternwheel steamers at dockside. In the foreground, right is the tug **DEFENDER**, and immediately to her stern, the venerable steamer **NORTHERN LIGHT**, which ran between Olympia and Shelton.

Pioneer steamer, the handsome sidewheeler **ANCON**, established a regular service between San Francisco, Puget Sound and Alaska in 1886, returning to the Sound on her first voyage with some $35,000 in gold. The **ANCON** was created out of an early day coal hulk at Panama. Rebuilt at San Francisco in 1873 for the Pacific Coast Steamship Co., the 266 foot liner was valued at $100,000, and gave a good account of herself until going on the rocks at Loring, Alaska while leaving the port, August 28, 1889. Captain D. Wallace was in command.

Alaska-bound aboard the steamer **ANCON** in the 1880's, as pictured in this classic view taken from a glass negative. It reminds one of staring into an old stereopticon. Evidently, the passengers paid little attention to the rules, as the sign on the housing, lower right, reads; "Passengers not allowed on top of this house." Who's that dapper fellow peaking out through the window at the bottom of the photo?

Half-scow, half-steamer, this disreputable appearing conveyance, the **ALKI,** was built at Seattle before the turn of the century for Captain M.D. McCall. She went anywhere a buck could be made on the Skagit, Snohomish, and on calm days, as far as Utsaladdy on Camano Island. Photo was taken about the turn of the century.

Seattle in the late 1870's showing the old railroad trestle across the mudflats of Elliott Bay which led up to the coal mining district, southeast of the town. At center, left, is the old Yesler Mill, with two sailing vessels waiting to load. At the far left, along the waterfront, an area later filled in, is the present site of the new Seattle sports stadium.

Mrs. H.G. Seaborn, sponsor of the SS **WEST HOBOMAC,** one of the 8,800 ton, 410 foot frieghters turned out by the Skinner & Eddy Corp. during World War I. Ship was built in only 49 working days. Note the star-bedecked launching platform.

Baptism by water, the SS **WEST ALSEK** built by the Seattle firm in 57 working days.

The Anderson Shipbuilding Company at Houghton as it appeared on March 14, 1918. The place later became the Lake Washington Shipyards. Below, the automobile ferry **LINCOLN** of Kirkland (built in 1914) is seen being overhauled. Courtesy Captain Bob Matson.

Chilean bark **BELFAST**, at a ballast dumping grounds on Puget Sound. The handsome square-rigger, built in England in 1874 for T. & J. Brocklebank, was the fastest unit of the company fleet, and at 260 feet in length was considered a very sizable ship in her day, a splendid sea boat. Sold to Shaw, Savill in 1901, she passed to Chilean operators in 1906 and spent the remaining 18 years carrying lumber from Puget Sound and nitrate from the west coast of South America, mostly under Captain Parajow. Lower, crewmen in the ship's hold shoveling ballast out to make room for cargo.

Port Townsend's waterfront in the 1890's was the scene of much activity, sailing vessels from all over the world calling at its port. Among them were many "hellships" whose empty berths were filled by unsuspecting sailors frequenting local "mad houses" and "gin mills." Others were shanghaied from boarding houses along the waterfront. Before the turn of the century much of this type of practice was curtailed, though the unsavory reputation of Puget Sound's "little Barbary Coast" lived on. Redding's Studio photos.

Two early views of Port Townsend, perhaps in the gay nineties, showing cross sections of the city with many vessels at anchor in the harbor. Some of the ornate buildings still stand today. Redding's Studio photos.

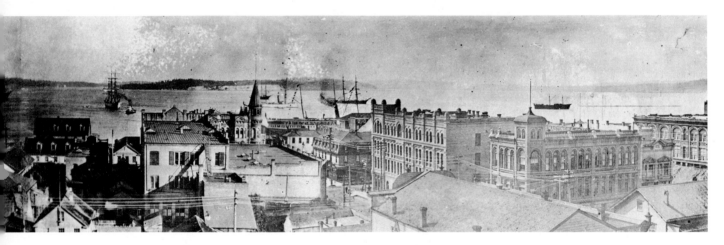

Idle sailing ships line Eagle Harbor waiting repairs, probably about 1910. At far left is the famous square-rigger **BENJ. F. PACKARD,** built at Bath, Maine in 1883. Another sailing vessel is on the drydock in the background.

A portion of Port Townsend's harbor as it appeared in 1900; several government vessels are swinging on their hooks. Redding's Studio photo.

Four-mast steel bark **LYNTON** of London, anchored in Port Blakely harbor. Built in 1894 in England, and commanded by K. A. Ekblom, the 2,531 ton vessel under owner R. Mattson, was later registered at Mariehamn, Finland, one of the meccas for tall square-riggers up through the 1930's.

One of the most often seen Webster & Stevens photos of early Port Blakely is this shot of the forecastle section of the schooner **BLAKELY** alongside a square-rigger, amid a wild array of ropes, shrouds, blocks and tackle, masts and yardarms.

Salty crew of a tall sailing vessel take to the rigging and yardarms to pose for a photo on a peaceful Puget Sound day. The canvas, hanging limp, is drying in the sun. The date was probably about the turn of the century.

Such scenes relegated to another time and another era can't help but stir the imagination, even of the landlubber. This photo was taken well before the turn of the century on Bellingham Bay, as a host of windships wait to take on lumber or coal.

Vintage photo of sizeable timbers being stacked on the Port Gamble mill dock, well before the turn of the century.

Sailing vessels waiting to load lumber at the Port Gamble mill, probably about 1890. The three-masted schooner is the **JOHN G. NORTH,** 336 tons, built on Coos Bay in 1881. The bark to the left is believed to be the **PACTOLUS,** a veteran 1,204 ton Downeaster, constructed at Thomaston, Maine in 1865.

Ah! what a sight for sore eyes. The picture tells the story. This is the historic mill at Port Gamble which dates back to 1853, and though modernized is still in operation, one of the only pioneer facilities to defy tide and time. Huge fir logs wait to go to the mill saws as four picturesque sailing vessels take on timber over their sterns. Photo taken around the turn of the century.

Two Boy Scouts gaze down from Magnolia Bluff in Seattle, as a three-masted bark lies silently at anchor. One can imagine the thoughts that are passing through their minds.

Norwegian iron hull bark **AUSTRALIA** outbound from Puget Sound in days of yore. Built in 1886, the 1,284 ton vessel was owned by Rasmus F. Olsen, and built at Bergen.

Peacefully moored on the Seattle waterfront, the bark **GLADYS**. The ramp, or trestle way to the vessel's stern is for sluicing Denny Hill. Note the beautifully carved figurehead on the **GLADYS**, a vessel owned by the Taltal Shipping Co. of Bristol, England. She was built at Bristol in 1891.

Launching of the cruiser **MILWAUKEE** at Tacoma. In 1923 the Todd Shipyard, at the city of destiny, completed three scout cruisers for Uncle Sam's Navy. The 550 foot, 7,500 displacement ton vessels added a new dimension to postwar shipbuilding on Puget Sound. In addition to the **MILWAUKEE**, were the scout cruisers **OMAHA** and **CINCINNATI**. The two tugs aiding the just launched **MILWAUKEE**, in the foreground, (upper photo) are the **HERO** and **WASP**.

Spoils of war. Often referred to as "Wilson's Wood Row," these photos show a vast surplus of World War I built, wooden hulled freighters that could find no employment after hostilities had ended. With stacks removed, they were lined up in long rows on Lake Union and other backwater moorages on Puget Sound, ending up in a funeral pyre or under the wrecker's hammer. Most were Ferris and Hough designs. Far left, (in upper photo) is the SS **KITAN**, a Ferris type steamer.

This is how it was in the late 1920's and early 1930's at the Port of Tacoma as scores of cargo vessels arrived to load lumber and other miscellaneous products for export. Seen in this photo, are Japanese, British and Dutch vessels loading for both the Orient and Europe.

Standard Oil tanker **RICHMOND** at the Standard Oil Co. dock on the Seattle waterfront, probably in the 1920's. Harbor Island is in the background.

Chapter Three
How Commerce and Industry Came To Be

*The bread earned by the sweat of the
brow is thrice blessed bread, and it is
far sweeter than the tasteless loaf
of idleness.*
                                  —Crowquill

T𝚘 𝚝𝚑𝚎 H𝚞𝚍𝚜𝚘𝚗'𝚜 B𝚊𝚢 C𝚘𝚖𝚙𝚊𝚗𝚢 credit must go for the initiation of commercial and industrial activities on Puget Sound. Even before opening a trading post at the southern limits of the inland sea, their curtain opener took place at Fort Vancouver on the Columbia River as early as 1826, with the establishment of a sawmill, grist mill and forge, built around a tiny fortress. In 1833, the company established Fort Nisqually on the southern fringes of Puget Sound which was to become the pioneer port of clearance for domestic and foreign trade. Importing supplies and selling them to territorial pioneers was the name of the game, while in turn, the produce of the settlers was shipped through the trading post to other markets.

By 1846, a grist mill, the first on Puget Sound was in operation at Tumwater, where Colonel Michael T. Simmons and his associates used stone burrs removed from a nearby stream to facilitate the operation. Six years later, Nicholas De Lin built a barrel factory, brewery, salmon packing plant and sawmill at Steilacoom. Small shipbuilding yards to turn out vessels to carry the produce and to service various Sound ports, began to rise from small clearings in the forested shores. One of the first was at Whidbey Island where in 1852, Captain Thomas Coupe turned out several small schooners at a place that came to be known as Coupeville.

Shipping from Puget Sound had an inauspicious beginning. Yankee ships had been infrequent callers since Captain Robert Gray's time, but in 1849 things began to happen. On November 23, 1849, the ship *Inez,* Captain Mosher, arrived at Nisqually, at least her boat crew did; the ship was tidebound below the narrows. She had come seeking a cargo of shingles, which had been purchased by Colonel Simmons at Fort Nisqually. Finally arriving at the fort December 5, she was joined the next day by another ship, the *General Patterson,* Captain Croser, which arrived with a cargo of supplies for the fort. In turn Croser was offered $1,000, by Dr. William Fraser Tolmie, a Hudson's Bay official, to transport a thousand live sheep to Victoria. He, however, declined and sailed without them — must have been alergic to wool. On February 23, 1850, the Yankee bark *Pleiades*, was in the area taking on logs, and the *Sacramento* was nearby loading both logs and shingles. Things were happening.

Early in January 1850, the brig *Orbit* sailed into Budd's Inlet, as far as she could make it toward the little settlement of New Market, (Tumwater) and then dropped her hook. Hailing from Calais, Maine, she had brought a number of gold-thirsty passengers out to San Francisco before coming to Puget Sound. In command of Captain William H. Dunham, she called at Fort Nisqually, requesting an Indian pilot to New Market. A wise old Indian piloted the brig to her destination where Colonel Isaac N. Ebey, met the vessel, and eventually purchased her with backing from B. F. Shaw, Edmund Sylvester and a man named S. Jackson. Thus the *Orbit* became the first ship owned outright on Puget Sound and forerunner of a vast fleet of American flag ships operated from Sound waters. Captain Dunham should have stayed with her, for after joining settlers and taking a claim on Chamber's Prairie, the following year was thrown from a horse and killed. Meanwhile, his former command, the *Orbit,* went on making money for her owners.

Meanwhile, larger vessels continued to arrive in greater numbers from San Francisco, bringing in the supplies for the little settlements, and departing with lumber, hides or fish. Trade became brisk with items selling at Olympia at $1.50 a bushel for potatoes; flour for $20 per hundred pounds; eggs 75 cents a dozen; butter at $1 per pound; molasses 75 cents a gallon; axes $2 to $8; sperm oil $1.50 per gallon, and candles 62 to 75 cents a pound — tabs somewhat akin to the inflationary prices of our times. Other imported items were Franklin stoves, clothing, tools, tinware, plows, paint, medicine, books, boots, glass and cutlery.

The potential value of commerce was at last an accepted reality on Puget Sound, a place where a short time earlier the only trade was Indian bartering. How fast things changed as the curtain opened on the second act with its new actors and actresses, for as it has been said, ''life is only a drama of dreams; its at first that it starts, each one plays a part, then fate chooses for us it seems.''

Lumber, fish and finally coal continued as the leading exports from Sound waters; only the fur trade diminished as the pelt bearing creatures were wantonly exploited at the hands of the greedy.

A massive barrier known as the Cascade Range divided Eastern and Western Washington and it was many years before the passes were conquered. Everytime a small gold or mineral strike of some kind was found on either side of the range, little settlements would start up, along with fresh talk about a rail line over the pass. But, many rich veins petered out before a year or two had passed, the surrounding villages reverting to ghost towns.

There, however, was no way of holding back progress on Puget Sound. From 1860 till the end of the century, it was sort of like a chess game, each town trying to out maneuver the other. Many of the most promising places made the wrong moves, while some of the least considered made all the right moves — sort of like the Bible says — ''the first shall be last and the last first.''

One town that started out like a whirlwind, is little more than a quiet memory today. Port Blakely on Bainbridge Island, not far from Restoration Point, where on May 29, 1792, the crews of Captain Vancouver's *Discovery* and *Chatham* celebrated, in picnic fashion, the anniversary of the restoration of King Charles II to the English throne.

Port Blakely grew around a huge lumber mill, which in time became the world's largest producer of soft lumber. It all started when Captain William Renton, seeking

Taking on flour at the Novelty Mill Co. below the slopes of West Seattle, back when. Moored to the dock is the innovative coastal gas-powered schooner **ANVIL**, which made occasional trips to Puget Sound but which did most of her work between Portland and Oregon coastal ports. Built at San Francisco in 1905, she featured portable berths for passengers in addition to her capacity for 300 tons of freight.

Wide-angle view of the dredging and preliminary construction site of the Pacific Steamship Company slip at Atlantic Street in Seattle, later Piers 36-37.

pilings for a customer in Boston, went ashore to develop the lumber business, and by 1864, had a mill going that was producing 50,000 board feet a day. This figure increased with the years as did the scope of the operation. The New England style town of Port Blakely grew up around the mill, with stores, churches, a public hall and a charming 75 room hotel. In the sawdust and plank streets and board sidewalks, prominent industrialists rubbed elbows with swarthy sailors and loggers. The 80,000 acre mill tract was served by 35 miles of rail line with four steam engines hauling timber on 100 cars. The Port Blakely Mill Company (Renton, Holmes and Co.) in its heyday employed 1,200 workers and cut some 400,000 board feet a day, a really flourishing enterprise. There was no unemployment in the town, in fact anyone that wasn't working was looked upon with contempt. If not working at the mill, the nearby shipyards employed several in turning out scores of wooden-hulled sailing vessels. It was in 1881, that the recognized Hall brothers, who had been operating a yard at Port Ludlow (site of another lumber mill) were induced to move their operations to Port Blakely setting up a facility that was unsurpassed on Puget Sound.

In 1888, the port was struck by a devastating fire, but the mill was rebuilt and kept on producing. As forests reserves began to dwindle logs were barged in from greater distances. During the town's apex, Port Blakely was visited by the President of the United States, the honorable Rutherford B. Hayes, who held office from 1877 till 1881. The streets and sidewalks were festooned with flags and bunting to honor the occasion, and all work ceased at the town establishments and business enterprises.

The downfall of Port Blakely was almost as rapid as its rise to fame. Where once crowds of tall sailing ships from all over the world gathered in the little harbor to load lumber and piling, the operation continued through the World War I era and was then slowly reduced, as Blakely became a quiet settlement with a few scattered family homes remaining with the ghosts of the vivid past.

Aside from the Port Blakely mill, the one enterprise that helped mold the town's rise to prominence was the Hall Bros. shipyard. Founded at Port Ludlow in 1874, the sparkplugs were Isaac, Winslow and Henry Hall. Operations continued there until the move to Port Blakely, and from that year until 1903, some 96 deepwater sailing vessels and a dozen steamers were constructed, all master-crafted, considered the finest of their type in the world — all wooden construction. Following the 1903 completion of the five-masted schooner *George E. Bil-*

A similar view of the Pacific Steamship Terminal at Atlantic Street, several months later. Note construction well underway on the office building, and the trackage. Albertson Cornell & Walsh were the contractors. This was the Seattle terminus for the famous Admiral Line ships such as the **H. F. ALEXANDER, EMMA ALEXANDER, RUTH ALEXANDER, DOROTHY ALEXANDER** and numerous others. The year, 1925.

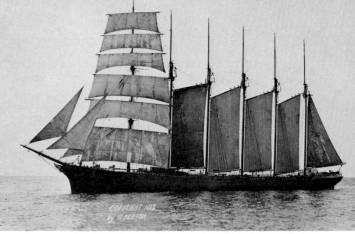

What a nostalgic sight this is, as the American Mail Liner, **PRESIDENT GRANT** departs her Smith Cove dock outbound for the Far East. There was a time, about 1923, when Seattle briefly was the largest passenger ship port on the West Coast, handling vessels going to Alaska, the Far East, coastwise and intercoastal. Today, only an occasional cruise liner calls, the airplane having put most passenger liners out to pasture, though the city does enjoy the Alaska State passenger ferries and the Washington State super ferries, which share the harbor with the new breed of cargo ships. American Mail Line, now a part of American President Lines of San Francisco, continues as a formidable carrier between the Pacific Northwest and the Orient.

One of the most interesting ship conversions ever undertaken on Puget Sound, was done at the Moran yard in Seattle in 1905. The hulk of the dismasted German four-mast bark **COLUMBIA** was purchased in British Columbia. One of the eight investors conceived the idea of rebuilding her with the rig of a six-masted barkentine. He was Captain J. W. Gibson. The completed vessel was named for another of the eight, **EVERETT G. GRIGGS.** Under Canadian registry she loaded lumber at Bellingham for Australia early in 1906, being the only vessel of her rig in the world. She later became the **E. R. STERLING,** and raised the Stars and Stripes. The vessel was originally built in 1883 as the British four-mast ship **LORD WOLSELEY.**

lings, the largest built by the firm, shipbuilding operations ceased at Port Blakely and the yard was moved a few miles north to Eagle Harbor where the Hall Bros. Marine Railway and Shipbuilding Company was established, with James Hall as its manager. There, numerous sailing vessels and steamers were repaired and some new ones built. The yard was later purchased by James Griffiths interests and years later, as the Commercial Ship Repair Co., continued to build small naval vessels during World War II. Now, though the town of Winslow continues to grow, the old yard is like so many others, a faded memory of the past.

Increasing coastal commerce demanded more and more ships, and by 1875 there were no less than 14 shipyards on Puget Sound, some tucked away in hidden coves dwarfed by great stands of fir, cedar and hemlock.

In that year alone, some 14 commercial sailing vessels and one steamer were completed, while annual exports of all kinds, were valued at $800,000.

By the year 1881 in Eastern Washington, Spokane was celebrating a great milestone when the first Northern Pacific train rolled into town. The territory was growing fast, and four years later Puget Sound was boasting of the fact that officially documented commercial vessels registered at its ports numbered 169, of which 80 were steam powered. The definite trend toward steam was becoming obvious, for in that same year (1885) of the 14 ships produced at local yards, eight were fitted with engines. In essence, it was the birth of the "mosquito fleet," which in years to follow was to become the lifeline of the inland sea, with a vast fleet carrying passengers, freight, mail and anything and everything else to and from every whistle stop that had anything that even resembled a dock. Wherever a buck was to be made they went, and competition was like hot embers.

Vintage photo taken at Vancouver B.C. harbor in 1891, shows two vessels that were well known on Puget Sound in the early days. At left, at dockside, is the steamer **PARTHIA,** one of the only existing photos of this vessel under that name. She later became the **VICTORIA** of the Alaska Steamship Co. and played a big part in the goldrush to Alaska. Originally, the vessel was built for Atlantic service for Cunard Line in 1870. To her stern is the infamous Canadian Pacific liner **Islander,** which struck an iceberg after departing Juneau, on August 15, 1901 and went to the bottom in Taku Inlet with the loss of 42 lives, including her master, Captain H. R. Foote. The photo was taken at the CPR Terminal in Vancouver.

Early photo of the docks at Bellingham, with the steamer **SEHOME** nudged in nose first. This 1902 scene, shows the steamer **NORTH PACIFIC** coming in for a landing, (in background) while in the foreground are seen the comical sidewheelers **ADVANCE** and the **TRIUMPH** which traveled up the Nooksack to several whistlestops. The old Whatcom Dock catered to a variety of Sound craft for many years.

In 1889, Washington became a full-fledged state, the 42nd to do so. The word territory was quickly left in the dust. Meanwhile back on the Sound, Tacoma and Seattle were slugging it out as to which would become the principal port city. By virtue of the early rail connection with the Columbia River, Tacoma gained an early edge, or if a play on words might be permitted — the inside track. But fate willed that Seattle would become the ''Queen City'' of Puget Sound while Tacoma, ''the City of Destiny,'' has continued to hang in there tough. One of the many factors that aided Seattle and the other larger ports of Puget Sound was the vital role played during the World War I era, when shipbuilding became a flourishing enterprise. Puget Sound yards constructed one quarter of all emergency freighters turned out for the United States Shipping Board. Never a day passed without a big steel freighter, a wooden-hulled cargo steamer or sailing vessel sliding down the ways, ships that played a big role in helping the United States turn the tide of the battle in favor of the allied cause. Even the dreaded German U-boat wolfpacks were unable to sink enough of the nation's emergency fleet to keep supplies from getting through.

Shipyards such as Skinner & Eddy, Duthie or Seattle Shipbuilding became household words and in no period of history did Puget Sounders become so maritime minded. As has long been said, American economy thrives best when on a wartime footing, when demand is the greatest.

With the cessation of hostilities, Seattle, along with the rest of the nation was hit by the postwar blues. Ships of every kind, type and description became a drug on the market. Backwater moorages were full and it was not

The classic old two-masted schooner **ECLIPSE** was the scene of many salty adventures of yesteryear. She is seen here at anchor in Port Townsend Harbor, a vestige of the past. Redding's Studio photo.

unusual to see a massive funeral pyre on an isolated Puget Sound beach where wooden-hulled ships had been purposely run aground. Saturated with combustibles the orange flames would leap high into the sky erasing in a moment what skilled men had labored long to build. The only recovery was the metal fittings gathered and melted down for use in another creation in another time and another place.

Not only shipbuilding, but most other segments of the economy fell into a state of lethargy. Many businesses ceased to be. On Puget Sound alone, some 3,000 factories

Port Madison, on Bainbridge Island probably in the 1890's, showing the residential section of the milltown. Founded in 1853 by G.W. Meigs, the town rose to a reputable place as an industrial center, for awhile serving as the county seat of Kitsap County. Today it is but a peaceful village, the mill long relegated to memory.

closed their doors. Revival was slow. It took fresh approaches and innovations in industry to get things moving again. Rising to the forefront was the food processing industry.

By 1929, the wheels of industry had been well oiled and in some cases were feeling the momentum of World War I days, with technological improvements and advanced manufacturing plants producing goods, not only for local consumption, but for overseas and domestic markets in increasing amounts. Production in the State approached $800 million in commodities, almost to the war-time level. Then, like a flash of lightning, the shovel broke. Almost overnight calamity hit the country. The bottom dropped out of the stock market. Striking with the suddenness of an aroused snake, the nation found itself in the depths of a great depression the likes of which it had never before known. Reaching into nearly every home and business, within a couple of years in Washington State alone, plants were off by 37 per cent of the 1929 totals. Many steamship lines that had served Puget Sound ports ceased operations or fell into bankruptcy. Soup lines grew longer. Sometimes activity on the local waterfronts of Puget Sound ports came almost to a standstill.

The Yankee ingenuity of being down but never out, prevailed. On the canvas till the count of nine, the nation's economy struggled through the early 1930's but gradually Puget Sound cities and towns fought their way back along with the rest of America.

World War II was a close reenactment of the first global conflict, only on a much more sophisticated basis. Everything boomed and though there was a small recession after the conflict ended, it was not as severe as in the wake of World War I. The rest of the story is already known. Who can say what the future will hold?

Looking back into Puget Sound industrial history, eying some of the natural resources that made it great before the transition, we again find at the top of the list, lumber. Even today, Oregon and Washington remain as the largest producers of soft timber in the United States, and though at the present time a large share of this commodity is exported in log form to Japan for processing, there was a time when lumber in various cuts filled the holds and decks of colorful sailing vessels, steam schooners and freighters traveling on coastal and intercoastal routes, while millions of board feet of ready cut lumber went out on scores of big cargo ships to most sectors of the world. Today it is packaged for shipment in containers while the coastwise lumber runs are handled by huge barges towed by powerful tugs.

As we earlier learned it was lumber that beckoned the pioneers to Puget Sound in the wake of the California goldrush. History records that Captain John Meares was

Eagle Harbor

Another early view of the Hall Bros. Marine Railway & Shipbuilding Company at Winslow on Eagle Harbor. Nearest camera is the big British sailing vessel **GANGES.** At center is the four-masted schooner **KITSAP** and the steamer **MONTICELLO.** Numerous other vessels line the harbor awaiting repairs.

Peaceful Eagle Harbor in the halcyon days of old.

Here is an overall view of Eagle Harbor, and the new Hall Bros. facility as seen in a wide angle camera lens. The yard is center left. Numerous sailing vessels and steam schooners line the bay. The view is from Winslow, named for Winslow Hall, who originally headquartered in San Francisco to get orders for the yard. Henry joined the partnership with his brothers in 1875. The Eagle harbor yard was established in 1903-04.

One of the largest World War I era shipyards in America was the Skinner and Eddy Corp. of Seattle. They specialized in 8,000 deadweight ton vessels starting in 1916 with three for Norwegian owners, and others for Japanese, French and British interests. After these ships were completed, the yard turned out 24 steel freighters of the "West" type for American flag service during the war and completed another 14, 9,600 tonners of the Edison type in 1919, as well as 19 of the Skinner and Eddy E.F.C. design during 1918-19. The yard was on the central Seattle waterfront. Note huge crowd on hand for the launching of one of the 412 foot steel cargo ships on July 17, 1918.

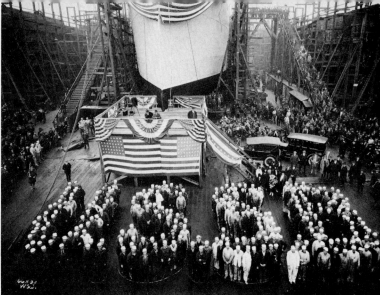

Last fling for wooden vessels of the large commercial variety was during World War I, when numerous Pacific Northwest shipyards were formed to meet the demands of world commerce in the war emergency. Here is a typical scene at the Elliott Bay Shipbuilding Company, formed in 1918, by veteran shipbuilder Clyde O. Morrow and capitalist Dr. C. A. Kilbourne. They received a contract from Scandinavian interests to build five 3,000 ton wooden motorships of the Coolidge design. Three were finished as intended, the others rigged as sailing vessels.

Launching of the SS **YUKON** at the Todd Drydock & Construction Co. in Tacoma, on October 26, 1918. The 4,843 gross ton cargo carrier was built for the United States Shipping Board. Note the yard workers spelling out USSB for the photographer. And, catch a glimpse of those jazzy automobiles.

first to export spars from Northwest waters, dating back to 1788. His destination was China but he encountered a North Pacific storm which necessitated the jettisoning of the cargo to save his ship. Captain George Vancouver was undoubtedly aware of Meares' experience, for when he was on Puget Sound four years later, he too was impressed with the value of the tall straight timber, replacing a broken spar (yardarm) on his ship with another, shaped from a choice Puget Sound log.

All of the early fur trading posts and fortresses were fashioned from the lumber hewn into shape from the readily available forests. As has been mentioned, in 1825, at Fort Vancouver on the banks of the Columbia, mill-wright William Cannon, whipsawed logs into boards, and the following year opened a mill with machinery imported from England. It was this same machinery that was later employed at the Puget Sound Milling Company at Tumwater.

As early as 1852, a cargo of piling was sent out to San Francisco from the Alki settlement, founded by the pioneers of Seattle. Mills were also started on Whatcom Creek and another at Tacoma, where a wooden water-wheel was turned by the flow from a ten foot dam, permitting the primitive facility to produce 2,000 feet of lumber daily.

By 1853, there were no less than 14 mills on Puget Sound run by the available water power, and another operated by steam. The latter was the first of its kind on Puget Sound, owned and operated by Henry Yesler and located at the tiny establishment of Seattle. This enterprising individual, one of the pioneer fathers of the future

city, sold his lumber from $200 to $500 a thousand feet.

Other mills were established at Appletree Cove in 1853, and the following year at Port Gamble where the Puget Mill Company (Pope & Talbot) has continued operations to this day, in a unique little town that has preserved the past with its vintage homes and buildings, some of which go back to the embryo years of the settlement. One feels like he is stepping back to a lost century when passing through. A movie production once used the town as a backdrop to represent an old New England seaport town.

Another early mill was located at Tulalip Bay where after a tribal reserve was established in 1857, the Indians were granted ownership and proved themselves fully capable of the responsibility by keeping it in operation for a half century. The turnover was one of the few humane dealings accorded the Indian in the wake of the Puget Sound treaties.

One of the most vexing problems of the early lumber-jacks and mill owners was the handling of the huge fir trees which often exceeded 200 feet in height with some 12 feet of girth. River drives were impractical, necessitating the pulling of logs over crude skidroads formed of short parallel timbers, well imbedded in the ground. By greasing them with stinky dogfish liver oil, a dozen oxen pulling as a team could pull tremendous weights. It was a smelly but effective operation. Most every part of the log found a use in early times. Even the tough, old tree roots were fashioned into coveted ship's knees, durability unlimited. Spars found international acceptance, big orders coming in from such buyers as the Imperial Spanish Navy.

A very early photo, (pieced together) of the Port Gamble mill. It was founded by Captain W. C. Talbot and A. J. Pope, J. P. Keller and Charles Foster, of East Machias, Maine, who fitted out the schooner **JULIUS PRINGLE,** a 50 ton craft in June 1853, for the express purpose of finding a suitable mill site on the Sound. Their choice — Port Gamble, just east of the peaceful waters of Hood Canal.

In 1864, after Congress granted to Northern Pacific Railroad all odd sections of land in a 40 mile strip of its planned trackage in the territory, it prompted the company to incorporate a land company to administer it and this tended to spur more lumber production.

By 1880, some 1,700 persons were employed in the lumber industry in Washington Territory, as new power equipment eased the burden of production. At Marysville, near Everett, the first logging locomotive was turned out in 1883 and rattled over a maple wood track. The donkey engine made its appearance on Bellingham Bay in 1887. In the same year, aided by new rail connections, the Territory's total production came to 645 million board feet, more than half of the output coming from Puget Sound. High lead logging was introduced near Port Townsend in 1896, followed a few years later by "skyline" logging. The name Weyerhaeuser then came on the scene, a name that was to become associated with a multimillion dollar enterprise which even today (headquartered near Tacoma) is one of the state's largest industries, with branches the world over.

A previously mentioned pioneer mill at Appletree Cove, was started by J. J. Felt during the cold winter of 1852-53, and by spring of the latter year was well into operation, much of the produce being exported on ships owned by the mill. George A. Meigs purchased the installation and moved it to Port Madison, on Bainbridge Island, but no sooner was the new mill producing than a spark of flame ignited causing a conflagration that leveled it in its entirety. But, Meigs was not a quitter and quickly rebuilt, doing bonanza business from 1854 until 1861. Port Madison became one of the more prosperous towns on Puget Sound, on a par with Steilacoom and Olympia, boasting a blacksmith shop, carpenter shop, a brass and iron foundry, machine shop, a general store, a church, school and a smattering of homes. In addition, just opposite the mill was a small shipyard. With lumber selling at from $200 to $500 per thousand feet, there was prosperity.

The Puget Mill Company's Port Gamble operation as it appeared in the fall of 1889. The vessels in the foreground appear to be sailing vessels cut down to barges.

Present day Port Gamble no longer has tall sailing ships crowded into its docks to load lumber, but on occasion a large cargo ship berths to lift the equivalent of that carried by a half dozen ships of old. The Pope & Talbot mill goes on producing, and the little town of Port Gamble is one of the best examples of the old New England style construction to be found anywhere west of the Rockies. Many of the original structures of the pioneer years still stand, and it is like stepping out of the present into the past when one enters the town limits. Joe took this photo of Port Gamble and the Pope and Talbot Mill in 1975.

Nor did Meigs stand for any nonsense in his town, it being one of the most orderly on the inland sea. He and the officials of the mill took a firm stand against wine, women and song sought after by the sailors on the many ships anchored in the bay awaiting lumber. The tough element that preyed on seafaring men tried to get a foothold, but Meigs ran the mill town in disciplined New England style. Though sometimes it came to a showdown, the worldly clan were finally forced to retrench at Port Blakely, which had the reputation of a wide open town. A large part of the mill's output of lumber went to San Francisco in Meigs' own ships which gave added profit to the operation, but there were also the square-riggers of many flags that loaded for most every port in the world.

Then again, that old demon fire struck the mill, this time on May 21, 1864. The flames spread so rapidly that only a miracle saved the ships loading at the dock and the entire town from destruction. That miracle was in the form of a wind that contain the fire at the millsite, giving the sailing vessels a chance to work free to an anchorage in the harbor.

Again Meigs put the broken pieces together. From the still warm embers the mill was reconstructed and within a few short months back in full operation. By 1872, Meigs had taken in a partner, William H. Gawley, of San Francisco and the firm name was changed to Meigs & Gawley.

Typical of the elegant old structures that stand against the march of time is the St. Paul's Church in Port Gamble, open for prayers and meditation at all times. Elegantly maintained, the old wooden structure is seen here on a crisp, winter day framed by tree branches, much as were the old churches of Maine, home of the mill's founders back in 1853. In this photo, Joe caught the nostalgic feeling one gets on visiting Port Gamble.

The unique old Puget Hotel, built at Port Gamble in 1903, though not one of the town's pioneer structures, was panelled with carved oak, mahogany, and rosewood shipped out years before the hotel was built. The beautiful yard with trimmed green lawn, and gorgeous flower beds set among tall maples and cherry trees, made the hotel one of the grandest places to visit in all the state. Note the period furniture and elegant woods. The hotel was still in business till recent times and it was a sad day when it was finally razed.

The new partner, however, suddenly became enthralled with mining and heavily invested the company revenues in mining stocks. By virtue of Gawley's unfortunate investment, the mill suffered a genuine setback during the national panic of 1873. Despite the blow, which almost wiped out the lumber operation, Meigs again rose like the proverbial phoenix, and four years later after taking in other investors, reorganized as the Meigs Lumber and Shipbuilding Company. Business once again flourished for several more years until Puget Sound giants combined to limit supply, causing Port Madison to virtually pass into oblivion.

The history of the Puget Mill Company at Port Gamble somewhat rivaled that of Port Madison except that it was destined never to close shop. It was founded by W. C. Talbot and A. J. Pope of San Francisco, along with J. P. Keller and Charles Foster, of East Machias, Maine. Fitting out the schooner *Julius Pringle*, in the early summer of 1853 at Frisco town, the small party sailed northward to seek a suitable millsite on Puget Sound. Captain Talbot commanded the vessel. Arriving at Port Discovery on July 14, they readied for the venture into Sound waters. Eventually the party settled on a spot rimming the east side of Hood Canal near its entrance, a place the Indians called Tekaleet. Thus it was that Port Gamble was founded. On September 4, 1853, the schooner *L. P. Foster*, Captain Keller, arrived after a 158 day passage from Boston with two steam sawmills and general merchandise for the settlement. By January 1854 the completed mill was operat-

Lumber stacked high at the Bryant's Mill waiting to be loaded aboard the steam schooner **SANTA ANA**, for down coast destinations. The **SANTA ANA**, a veteran lumber drougher, was built at Marshfield, Oregon in 1900, and traded along the coast for four decades.

Transition period between steam and sail is noted on the Seattle waterfront several decades back. The two steamers in the foreground are the liner **UMATILLA** of the Admiral Line and the freighter **REDONDO**, of Alaska Steamship Co. At the pierside right, are the four-masted schooner **HENRY WILSON** and the bark **GEORGE CURTIS**.

Three's company. A trio of American Hawaiian Steamship Company cargo ships in dock at the same time on the Seattle waterfront, probably in the late 1920's. From left, the steamships **OHIOAN, OREGONIAN** and **VIRGINIAN**. Harbor Island is in the background.

Port Ludlow, on the west shores of Puget Sound was once a flourishing mill town, but today has become the site of a luxury resort featuring condominiums and vacation property. The mill, seen at the extreme left, shows the old brick smokestack around which the mill was built. The original mill was the first in Jefferson County, founded by eager William F. Sayward and J. F. Thorndyke. For many years it was a leading producer on the Sound catering to scores of sailing vessels. When the mill was updated in 1883, the historic Admiralty Hotel was built in the town of Port Ludlow, catering to many VIP's down through the years. It remained till the 1940's. Ferries formerly landed at Port Ludlow, and before the ferryboats, little steamers of the mosquito fleet.

ing 13 saws. In March, in addition to cut lumber, shingles were also being produced. Meanwhile the *Foster* took on a full cargo of lumber, the first to be exported from the facility, which was organized as the Puget Mill Company.

Port Gamble has lived on into the nuclear age. In its early history company executives wisely bought up big timber acreage from the government at from $1.25 to $2.50 per acre. By the turn of the century it had 100,000 acres and by 1880 the annual output of sawed lumber was some 36 million board feet. Cyrus Walker managed the mill for several years and in 1876, the Pope & Talbot interests purchased the mill at Utsalady on Camano Island, and again two years later, the Port Ludlow mill which was then producing 150,000 board feet a day.

The stately appearing Admiralty Hotel at Port Ludlow which catered to many executives and celebrities during the boom years of the lumber mill. The structure lasted till the 1930's and then slowly slipped into oblivion along with the rest of the town. A resort marks the locale today. Courtesy Redding's Studio, Port Townsend.

There was excitement at Gamble in 1889, when the partly unloaded bark *Emerald* caught fire at the lumber wharf. Quick action by her master, Captain A. Ford, his crew and the mill hands saved the mill, but the 34 year old New York-built bark was a total loss.

Captain William Renton, and Charles C. Terry, constructed a small steam mill at Alki in 1853 but soon moved its equipment to what they believed to be a more promising site at Port Orchard, just across Sinclair Inlet from the present site of Bremerton. In 1854, the first large export cargo of lumber was dispatched to San Francisco aboard the brig *Leonesa*. Captain Renton sold out to Colman & Falk in 1862 and they continued operations for several years. The mill was rebuilt in 1869, but by then the lumber market had gone sour for a spell, and financial disaster struck. Company property and its ships were seized by the authorities and sold at auction to pay accumulated debts. The curtain closer came in 1870 when the mill and much of the town burned. Some said the fire was started by a disgruntled arsonist, but whatever the reason, the mill never again rose from the ashes and the town to this day has remained small though still the county seat.

Again we return to Captain Renton, who after having long before sold out his interest in the Port Orchard operation went to San Francisco and returned with machinery, boilers and engines for a new mill at Port Blakely. A brief mention of Captain Renton was made earlier in this writing but to continue our thumbnail history of the lumber industry we take up with this enterprising squire. It is of interest to note that he and a handful of his followers on

A lumber mill was started on the Whatcom River near Bellingham as early as 1853, by Captain Edward Eldridge, William Brown, Henry Hewitt and William Utter, after lumber prices in the wake of the San Francisco fire sent prices skyrocketing to $1,000 a thousand board feet. By the time the mill was producing, the price fell to $20 per thousand; a hard pill to swallow. In later years, steam operated equipment was installed at Bellingham logging and lumber sites, as seen here. In 1854, Captain Roeder, built the small schooner **H.C. PAGE** to carry lumber to the outside world from Bellingham Bay. Later coal outcroppings were discovered in the area, affording a double industry to attract capital to the greater Bellingham area, which was a composite of the towns of Fairhaven, New Whatcom and Sehome.

surveying the new site of their Port Blakely mill sounded the depths of the harbor with an iron tied to a piece of clothesline. Only then were they satisfied that it was deep enough to accomodate the sailing vessels that would soon be coming in to load. Cutting at the mill began in April, 1864 and the initial cargo was shipped to San Francisco on the bark *Nahumkeag*. By 1879 the average capacity was some 20 million board feet per year.

In 1868, the official name of the firm was Renton, Smith & Company, but six years later it was changed to Renton, Holmes & Company, the faithful bookkeeper, C. S. Holmes having been taken into the partnership. Business flourished and at one time during the life of the plant there were as many as 40 sailing vessels and steamers crowded into the small harbor. Lumber was stacked high on the docks but the stock piles dwindled quickly into the hungry holds of the scores of ships.

A disastrous fire hit the mill in 1888 but like the Port Gamble revival, so it was with Mr. Renton's prosperous facility. Again from the ashes the mill was rebuilt. Though located on an island, the domestic produce was towed to the mainland and tugs which connected with a logging railroad, built in the early 1880's with company funds operated all the way to the Chehalis Valley, often bringing raw logs to water side.

As early as 1857 an active little mill began producing lumber at Seabeck on Hood Canal. Second-hand machinery was shipped north from San Francisco by company principals — J. R. Williamson, W. J. Adams, W. B. Sinclair and Hill Harmon. Some 50,000 feet was cut daily and nearly all of it went out to foreign ports.

Sailors and lumbermen flocked into Kitsap County, for the larger share of the pioneer lumber mills were located within its boundaries. For a short while Kitsap was one of the most populated counties on Puget Sound and at one time outdid all others, mostly due to its mills and shipyards.

Doing it the hard way. This is one of the early day primitive Northwest sawmills, where rugged men put in a 12 hour day without fringe benefits.

W. P. Sayward and J. R. Thorndike built the sawmill at Port Ludlow in 1853 and within two months of their arrival the saws were cutting. Five years later Amos Phinney & Company leased the plant for $500 per month, but in 1866 it failed. Many left the little settlement, but eight years later reorganization came about under the name Port Ludlow Mill Company, the property then being sold to Puget Mill for $64,000. With Cyrus Walker, a man of great inititive as manager the production was upped to 150,000 board feet a day, and Port Ludlow was back on the map.

In 1857, at the north end of Camano Island at a spot called Utsalady, the frame for a sawmill was erected. Sawing began the following year, although Thomas Cranney, partner of Lawrence Grennan in the development of the little port, had earlier shipped out (1856) a cargo of spars aboard the Dutch ship *Williamsberg*. Utsalady, little more than a ghost town today, means in the Indian tongue, "land of berries," but its founders had visions of it growing much more than a stack of berries, and for awhile it showed great promise. Cranney and his partner Grennan had visions of a dream city. In fact, even before the town was founded, Grennan and two earlier partners named Thompson and Campbell, chose the sight for logging operations. With deep water in the small harbor and virgin

Water transportation along with the city undergo transition. This is the Seattle waterfront back in the halcyon days of the late 1920 period showing the steamship **VICTORIA**. The old Colman dock with its giant clocks is at right and the tall tower just behind the ship's pilothouse is the Grand Trunk Pacific dock. The **VICTORIA**, built in Scotland in 1870, as Cunard's SS **PARTHIA**, later came west to play a starring role during the goldrush days, and to become the "darling" of all the Alaska Steamship Company passenger liners. Note the buildings up town and then compare them with the scene below, taken in 1974, showing the fantastic changes. The **SEA LAND COMMERCE,** of Sea-Land Service, largest container ship line in the world, is off to the Far East with hundreds of containers filled with a variety of cargo. By comparison, the **SEA LAND COMMERCE,** is about three times as long as was the **VICTORIA.**

forests all about, production at the mill brought a large number of square-rigged ships to load lumber for Holland, France, England, Spain, China and Mauritius. Behind the millsite were warehouses, and even a ship agency. In the town was a hotel, a school, newspaper office, several residences, and along the shore, a small shipyard. But alas, it is all gone today, a smattering of beach residences leaving no traces of what used to be. Like one old timer put it, "It's strictly for the berries, jest like its Indian name sez."

Ah, but in the better days, say back in 1857-58 after Cranney had replaced Thompson as Grennan's partner, the mill was sending out cargoes of spars for the French, British and American navies, all within a single year. These select timbers, 100 to 125 feet in length and 30 to 50 inches in diameter at the stump, weighed up to

20 tons each and required skill in handling, especially with the primitive equipment then available.

The founders of Utsalady had actually begun operations at Penn's Cove on Whidbey Island from where piling was shipped to San Francisco. When Grennan saw the sturdy Douglas firs and deepwater anchorage on Camano Island, he purchased in February 1853, 160 acres of timber from S. D. Howe. For a short while in Utsalady's rise to fame, its principals and its citizens were talking of a rail link, a college and even a canal which would cut through nearby Whidbey Island to create a direct water route to their port. But talk is cheap. Grennan died in 1869, leaving Cranney in full command. One of the proudest boasts of the deceased was a flagstaff 150 feet long and 24 inches at the stump end which was shipped from the mill aboard the ship *Belmont* for display at the

Utsalady as it appeared in 1862. From an old lithograph in the Northwest collection at the University of Washington.

Paris Exposition. All the Frenchmen were asking: "Where's Utsalady?"

One of the frustrating occurrences in the early history of Utsalady was when Grennan first planned his sawmill. He ordered the equipment from San Francisco out of profits made from piling and salted salmon. The equipment was jettisoned, irretrievably lost when the vessel hauling it north stranded on the Columbia River bar. Grennan then returned to San Francisco and persuaded the machinery company to refill his order on credit. At about this juncture he took in Cranney as his partner.

Supplies for Cranney's store were brought north later from San Francisco on the bark *Anadyr*, owned and commanded by Captain James H. Swift of Coupeville. Outbound, the ship loaded a full cargo of Utsalady spars, clearing Port Townsend December 1, 1855 for Falmouth, England and Brest, France allegedly the first full cargo of spars ever to be exported from Puget Sound country, the exporters being Grennan & Thompson.

All dreams must come to an end. In 1876 the plant at Utsalady was sold to Puget Mill who carried on operations for two more decades, then closed it down and put a padlock on the door.

In the interim, J. R. Williamson disposed of his interest in the Seabeck mill to partners Adams and Blinn, and they together with Charles Phillips of Whidbey Island and Captain Plummer of San Francisco, built a mill on the west shore of Elliott Bay, near Seattle, starting operations in 1864 with an output of 50,000 board feet per day. Around it grew the little village of Freeport, today part of West Seattle. This plant was engulfed in fire in April 1867, but was back in production the following year.

At the head of Port Townsend Bay, Samuel Hadlock provided the financial backing, and a man named Glidden

The tug **WANDERER**, built at Port Blakely in 1890, is seen towing the bark **GANGES**. The tug which later did stellar work for the Foss Launch & Tug Company, is here operated by the Puget Sound Tug Boat Company.

Pilot boarding the bark **GANGES** on Puget Sound in the early years of this century. This vessel dating from 1882, when built at Sunderland, England was sold to Norwegian interests in 1904.

In these photos, deepsea freighters bring in pig iron shipments from China for discharge at the Irondale plant. Above, the SS **M. S. DOLLAR** prepares to discharge, while in the lower photo a foreign carrier unloads onto barges.

was hired to run a portable sawmill. An article appearing in the *Argus* in 1871 read: "The ship *Caroline Reed,* commanded by Captain John F. Hinds took a cargo from the Glidden mill this week. This is the first vessel to load on the bay since 1865, when the *Lucy Ann,* bark *Narramissic* and the brig *Sheet Anchor* loaded lumber at the Chimacum Creek Mill."

In 1858-59, a mill erected at Port Discovery by the S. L. Mastick & Company of San Francisco gave a good account of itself by producing six million feet per annum. The success of the operation became obvious after it doubled its output and then by 1874 tripled, with an annual figure of some 18 million board feet. Thereafter production gradually declined and today, only a few old pilings remain in the peaceful bay, like tombstones marking a watery grave.

David Livingston put a small mill into operation on the Snohomish River, three miles above its mouth in 1863 and used his own little steamer to tow logs and lumber to the area pioneers along the river bank. Earlier Roeder & Peabody, built still another at the mouth of Whatcom Creek on Bellingham Bay in the winter of 1852-53. It became a little money maker for two decades, but in 1873 was consumed in flames. Sometime later a new mill, equipped with steam power, was built on the same site. Other mills were erected on the Black River near the mouth of the Cedar River in 1853-54, but gold fever at Colville beckoned its founders, Fanjoy and Eaton who in turn locked shop and traveled to what they thought were greener pastures on the other side of the Cascades. Unfortunately, both were murdered by hostile Indians.

The now non-existent Commencement City, was the site of a small mill near Tacoma in October 1868, when Charles Hansen and John Ackerson of San Francisco found it was profitable to have sawdust in one's hair. Nobody much regarded this odd couple at first but suddenly they emerged as a top competitor, challenging even the Sound's lumber king — Renton's Port Blakely mill, with a cut of 250,000 board feet per day. It was a neck and neck race for a long time, but the Bainbridge Island facility finally nipped the maverick in the bud with its record output of 400,000 feet a day.

Until the 1880's all of the logs on the Sound were cut with axes and hauled to the millsites either over skidroads or on the water. It greatly speeded production when saws were utilized in the forests.

Forest fires were not uncommon in the pioneer era but the cause was not usually from careless campers or cigarette smokers, but moreso from lightning. Smokey Bear had little say. In the *Journal of Occurrences,* kept at old Fort Nisqually, there exists a record of disastrous forest fires as early as August 1835 and again in October 1836. The first account read: "The country around us is all on fire, and the smoke is so great that we are in a measure protected from the excessive heat." The second account in the record revealed: "The weather is gloomy from the smoke around us. The country around is all on fire."

Sometimes such fires would continue unchecked for a month or more until God sent a generous supply of rain. There is one early case of a ship going aground in the Strait of Juan de Fuca when an uncontrolled forest fire in the Olympics cast a lingering pall of smoke thicker than fog, that blotted out all land and seamarks. During such occasions the sun would be completely obliterated for days.

By 1900, Washington State had risen to fifth position among lumbering states, and five years later, by doubling production, occupied first place. By 1910, some four billion feet of lumber was being produced and within four years there were 912 mills employing about 38,000 persons. When the depression of 1929 struck, some 900 plants were employing 52,000 persons in the lumber industry with an annual value of $300 million. In the depres-

Pittsburgh of the West? Well, it started out all right, but the enterprise died a slow death after its promoter was drowned in the **CLALLAM** disaster on January 8, 1904. The steamer, after leaving Port Townsend sank in the Strait of Juan de Fuca in a severe storm. Some 54 persons drowned, including Homer H. Swaney, head of the Pacific Steel Company of Irondale, who had migrated west from Pennsylvania. The plant is shown here under full production.

Rolling steel ingots into billits at the Pacific Steel Company at Irondale around the turn of the century.

An early photo of Port Angeles with a government lighthouse tender at the dock face. The date was probably before the turn of the century.

sion years the industry declined, but in essence was actually undergoing a transition with by-product manufacturing such as plywood, pulp, paper products and a host of other specialty items. Many of the local forests dwindled before the axe and saw, from disease, fire and the demand for more and more land by an ever increasing population. Reforestation helped some, but the available stands were pushed farther and farther from the metropolitan areas. At

Port Angeles as it appeared in 1975 showing the waterfront resort facility and a log ship at dock, far left.

the same time, trains and trucks could go most anyplace to haul it out to distribution centers. Though the manufacture of lumber is still a factor on the Sound, it is not like the past decades when lumber vessels of many varieties were packing out on the coastwise and intercoastal runs. Much of the business has gone to the timber-rich areas of British Columbia. Most of the port cities from Port Townsend to Tacoma have flourishing pulp mills, but the odiferous operations are frequently a bane to sensitive noses.

A controversial export in modern times is the millions of tons of raw logs exported to Japan for processing, a movement that has greatly threatened the future of western Washington lumber reserves, not to mention those of Oregon. Inflation has hampered many of the local lumber mills though the demand continues great.

Several gold finds stirred excitement in the territory in the early years as did the discovery of other precious metals. One of the first gold strikes was near old Fort Colville, on the east bank of the Columbia River in 1855. But it wasn't gold and silver that were to become the most important to Puget Sound, but the non-metallic substances from the earth — coal, limestone, building stone, clay, etc. Coal made the biggest impact, numerous ships being attracted to Puget Sound ports in the early years to load out with the black substance.

Copper ores of varying types were found, basically in the Chewelah, Chelan and Index districts. The Tacoma Copper Smelter, a plant that started operation at Tacoma

One of the oldest known photos of Port Orchard, a town that put its roots into the ground in 1854 and which once boasted a flourishing pioneer lumber mill. For many years it was named Sydney, but in 1903 the name was changed to Port Orchard. Today it is the seat of Kitsap County. It looked like hardtimes when this picture was taken. Courtesy Mrs. Daily, daughter of the late Stewart Osborn.

in 1889 under financier, W. R. Rust is still very much a factor to this date. In more recent years its capacity was built up to about 50,000 tons of ore per month but the basic problem as far as the public is concerned has been the control of the smelly emission that often drapes itself over the city.

It was Dr. William Frazer Tolmie, a dominant factor in the Hudson's Bay Company who in 1833 called attention to the territory's coal deposits at the junction of the Cowlitz and Toutle rivers. Discoveries were also made on the Stillaguamish River in 1851, and a year later on the Black River near Renton. At the latter site, mining proved profitable inasmuch as the deposits were conveniently near the waters of Puget Sound.

The initial commercial shipment of Puget Sound coal

was through Bellingham Bay in the late 1850's. The cargo went by sailing ship to San Francisco. For the next two decades, Bellingham Bay was the principal export area for overseas coal. Big time King County coal mining was considered in 1863, when Lyman B. Andrews came to a Seattle assayer's office with a flour sack full of coal dug in the Issaquah area. Other deposits were found and mined at Newcastle, and on the strength of this, the Pacific Coast Coal Company was formed, and soon a rail line between Seattle and Newcastle became a reality. That was in 1875, and it gave a real shot in the arm to Seattle as a seaport. Of all the early coal finds in the territory, the Newcastle operation was the most successful. In 1880 Henry Villard of the Northern Pacific, organized the Oregon Improvement Company which acquired the mines and railroad,

Port Orchard's waterfront in the early 1920's showing the H. B. Kennedy Wharf and the Central Wharf. A battlewagon lies at anchor in the inlet and in the left background is seen the Puget Sound Naval Shipyard at Bremerton. Courtesy Mrs. Daily of Poulsbo.

Port Orchard main street — a host of the latest model autos parked in the center of the road, back in the World War I era. There have been many changes in the 50 years that followed. Courtesy Mrs. Daily of Poulsbo.

Dig that fancy metropolis of Port Blakely. Mill and shipyard workers have a day off, one of those days just right for a bicycle ride. Hard to tell the handlebar mustaches from the bicycle handlebars. This enterprising group is posing on Port Blakely's "famous" board walk.

and the production was brought up to 145,000 tons per year. To the amazement of fair goers at Chicago's Columbian Exposition in 1893, a 25 ton block of coal, from Northern Pacific's Roslyn mine, largest ever cut to that time, was put on display.

Despite an attempt by the state legislature to control monopolies, the big operators succeeded in crowding out most of the independents. By 1918, coal production in the state had passed the four million ton mark, and this bonanza continued through the 1920s until oil took over the throne as the "black gold" king of world commerce and industry. This turnover, of course, led to the quick demise of coal mines, and several more local ghost towns appeared.

Kittitas, King and Pierce counties respectively were the leaders in coal production, much of it being used for homes, factories, railroads, coke and gas manufacturing, and for bunkering ships. The remainder went out as export cargo. Someday, if the oil shortage becomes acute and other sources of energy are lacking, many of the old coal areas in Western Washington may again be activated. Western Canada mines have become very active in recent years, and much of its produce is being shipped directly to Japan to operate several of the larger plants in the land of the rising sun.

One of the nearly forgotten ports of Puget Sound is Irondale, on the western shore of Port Townsend Harbor about a mile from the head of the bay. It is the site of a former iron foundry that was to have added a whole new dimension to the state's economy. Billed as the future "Pittsburgh of the West," a small town sprang up around a huge blast furnace before the turn of the century. It produced pig iron made from raw ore shipped in from local sources and from the Orient. The "pigs" in turn were used both domestically and shipped to world wide destinations. There appeared a great future for Irondale but its demise was hurried when on the night of January 9, 1904, the steamer *Clallam* foundered in the Strait of Juan de Fuca with a loss of 54 lives, one of whom was Homer H. Swaney, guiding light behind the Pacific Steel Company of Irondale. A native of McKeesport, Pa., he had the financial backing of many of his former Pennsylvania business associates. He had visions of making Irondale the steel city of the west, but with his death, all contracts fell by the wayside, and the plant drifted into financial difficulties. It was soon sold and dismantled, robbing Port Townsend Harbor of another promising industry. Today, Irondale could hardly qualify as a village, and nothing remains of the old plant, except a few memories and alot of ghosts of the past.

Before the turn of the century, this was a typical scene at the Hall Bros. shipyard at Port Blakely on Bainbridge Island. Two wooden schooners are seen under construction in the background, right. Note the heavy, seasoned timbers.

The Hall Bros. shipyard looking toward the Port Blakely Mill Co., where a score of windjammers await cargoes of lumber. Note the factory houses rimming the waterfront. Now a ghost port, this is how things were before the turn of the century.

In those days it was the largest softwood lumber producing mill in the world — the Port Blakely Mill Co. — ships from all over coming to take on the precious cargo. Scenes such as this are relegated to faded memory. At the busy millsite, the veteran square-rigger **MERCURY,** owned by Renton, Holmes & Co. and registered at Port Townsend, awaits her cargo. Formerly a Havre packet, the **MERCURY** was built at New York in 1851. Note her ornate square stern.

Loading lumber at the Port Blakely Mill Co. are six sailing vessels of varying rigs, amongst which are found the British, German and American flags. Second and third from the left are the American flag four-mast schooner **BLAKELY** and the barkentine **NEWSBOY,** and at center, a big Hamburg bark.

Ready to load lumber, the picturesque 2,156 ton ship **BENJ. F. PACKARD** at the Port Blakely Mill dock. Note the ornate billet head and trailboards on this fine old wooden full rigger, turned out at Bath, Maine in 1883 by Goss & Sawyer.

Strolling down the old board walk at Port Blakely in the early days one would have seen at anchor tall Yankee wood-hulled ships, built as Downeasters, awaiting cargoes of lumber.

This picture taken in 1886, shows the sternwheeler **CASCADE** at dockside either at Stanwood or Fir. Built at Seattle in 1884, the steamer ran on many river routes. To her left is the Fir Hotel.

There was a trading post at La Conner as early as 1867, located on the Swinomish Slough. First named Swinomish, it was later renamed by the area's first permanent settler, John S. Conner for his wife, Louisa A. — thus La Conner. It is the home of the state's first newspaper weekly, and is across the slough from the Swinomish Indian Reservation. The accompanying scene shows an overall view of the interesting little town as it appeared in 1895. Nearby, on January 22, 1855, the chiefs of the Snohomish, Snoqualmie, Duwamish and allied tribes met at their Long House with Governor I. I. Stevens and ceded to the white men all land from Point Pully to the Canadian border, a sad day for the Indian.

Classic photo of the famous SS **PORTLAND** after being taken over in 1906 by Alaska Coast Company, a subsidiary of Pacific Coast Steamship Co. She had a long series of mishaps on the inside passage to Alaska, finally meeting her doom on November 12, 1910, in charge of Captain Franz Moore. Striking an uncharted rock, part of a reef near Katalla, she became a total loss. Gone she was, but never forgotten.

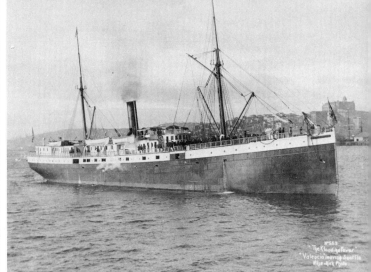

Came the Goldrush days, and ships by the score departed Seattle laden with gold seekers. Here is the steamer **OHIO** in heavy ice off Nome, Alaska. Lower photo. The same **OHIO**, a grim tombstone along the inside passage to Alaska. She was wrecked in Heikish Narrows August 24, 1909. A former Atlantic liner, dating from 1873, she joined the goldrush bonanza under the Empire Line banner and was later owned by Alaska Steamship Company.

Never was there so much excitement and activity on the Seattle waterfront as during the Alaska goldrush era. One of the ships that played a big role was the Pacific Coast Steamship Company's SS **VALENCIA,** which dated from 1882. The iron single screw steamer was purchased from the Pacific Packing & Navigation Company by the Pacific Coast Company in 1902, and just four years later while in the coastwise passenger service met a tragic ending by crashing ashore on the West Coast of Vancouver Island with the loss of 117 lives. In the upper photo, the old Washington Hotel can be seen atop Denny Hill. Below, the hosts of people on the dock took liberties on the SS **VALENCIA** to get in the photo.

Goldrush fury. A typical scene on the central Seattle waterfront in 1898 as the SS **OHIO** prepares to depart for Alaska. It will never be like that again. In the background is the old Schwabacher's Wharf.

This is what started it all. These are probably the only known photos of the "famous ton of gold" being discharged from the SS **PORTLAND**, the parcels that started the big stampede to the Klondike in 1897 and 1898. The lower photo is reputedly the **PORTLAND** arriving at her Seattle pier July 8, 1897. The gathering was due to a newspaper story that told of the gold, even though a few days earlier another ship with a like amount of gold had arrived at Seattle, virtually unnoticed. The change in the Seattle scene was almost instantaneous. It became the supply and embarkation center for thousands going north to seek their fortunes. The **PORTLAND**, a unit of the North American Transportation & Trading Co., has remained one of Seattle's immortal ships, for it was her arrival that opened an entire new era.

Chapter Four
If It Swims We Have It

Master, I marvel how the
fishes live in the sea.

      —Pericles

A FISH MARKET on the Seattle waterfront has long used the slogan, "If it swims we have it!" Indeed, Puget Sound has a large variety of fish and mammals and is a desirable haven for both commercial and sports fishermen. Sound ports are jumping off places for the North Pacific and Alaska fishing grounds. It is homeport for great hordes of salmon, the delicacy that tickles the taste buds of gourmets the world over. Washington ports continue as outfitting, processing and shipping headquarters for the North Pacific fishing industry and thousands of commercial fishing craft are registered at Puget Sound ports.

The popularity of Puget Sound as a fishing mecca began with the native Indian, who adopted the salmon as his most cherished food. Though he relished the other varieties of fish and crustaceans, nothing for him could replace sockeye, coho, humpback, pink, king and other varieties of Oncorhynchus, which is just another way of saying salmon.

When Captain Vancouver was on Puget Sound in 1792, he found the natives "fishing for salmon with crude nets made of bark and young willows." He further mentioned racks which they used for drying fish. Then there was the Indian weir, composed of several tripods of alder poles set up in a river or creek where the water was shallow, upon which a platform about six feet square held an Indian fisherman who "watched" with great patience. When the schools of fish congregated below him, he employed a long dip net to scoop out his catch.

In the mid 1850's, Puget Sound waters were literally teeming with fish and one needed no good luck charm to land a "big one," nor did he need to repeat the "Fisherman's Prayer," unless for spiritual purposes.

> God grant that I may live
> to fish until my dying day,
> And when my final cast is made,
> I most humbly pray when in the
> Lord's landing net, I'm peacefully
> asleep. That in his mercy I be
> judged good enough to keep.

In the early years of the 19th century when the North West Company established a post at the entrance to the Columbia River, near the site of Astoria, they introduced the salting process for preserving fish. Later, Hudson's Bay Company developed an export trade in sockeye salmon, quinnat, and isinglass (made from sturgeon) items which were transported to the Hawaiian Islands, Australia, Japan, China and to the Eastern

Fishing steamer **NEW ENGLAND**, built at Camden, N.J. in 1897. Veteran Puget Sound master mariner, Captain Ben Joyce, came around to Seattle as a member of the crew in March 1898. Built for the New England Fish Co., represented by Captain H.B. Joyce, the vessel was designed exclusively for halibut fishing in North Pacific waters, homeporting at Seattle.

Seaboard. Among the front runners who packed salt salmon on Elliott Bay for export to San Francisco were Chief Sealth (Seattle) and David Maynard. The biggest problem was when a ship was plagued by weather conditions that necessitated an extra long passage, causing spoilage. The taste buds however, prevailed, and before long, fish packers were operating small plants in various corners of Puget Sound.

As early as September 10, 1853, several men were catching salmon commercially at Point Roberts, a small peninsula of isolated American land jutting out from the British Columbia border. Four years later, pioneer John West began salting salmon in barrels on the Columbia River and was responsible for inventing the canning machine. In 1873, V. T. Tull began packing salmon at Mukilteo, and by 1877 the Jackson-Meyers Company had established the first full-fledged cannery on Puget Sound.

Whaling vessels based at Puget Sound ports went out after the big leviathans in past decades and this industry gained some impetus locally, but oils produced from dogfish and candlefish developed into a 60,000 barrel annual output.

With the completion of the Northern Pacific Railroad, it became possible to ship fish to Eastern and mid-western markets. The Pacific Packing and Navigation Company came west from New Jersey in 1901, with a capitalization of $32 million. Gaining control of several Puget Sound and Alaska operations, they found a profitable market.

In 1903, E. S. Smith patented the "Iron Chink," so named because it was designed to replace the work of cheap Chinese labor. Not that the Chinese were slack in their work, no way, but they were just no match for an invention that could butcher and clean 60 to 85 salmon a minute. It was a sad day for many an Oriental; for some, it was back to the proverbial Chinese laundry.

Commercial fishing progressed in 1903 when the first gas-powered purse seiner, the *Pioneer*, made its appearance. Before long, fishing scows vanished as did the steam powered fishing craft. In turn, scores of gas-powered seiners, trollers and trawlers frequented the ports of Puget Sound.

And, then of course there was the halibut business. An attempt was made about 1870 to export fresh ice packed halibut from Puget Sound to San Francisco via

In 1911, the Moran shipyard in Seattle completed the salty looking whale killer steamers **MORAN** and **PATERSON** for Canadian Fisheries Co. They were stationed at Ocosta, on Grays Harbor. The 12 knot steam powered craft hauled in 43 whales within their first month of operation.

sailing vessel, but the venture failed, so did the ice. Commercial halibut exports moving inland were not really successful until the railroad came through. The initial shipment of fresh halibut to the midwest was made from Tacoma by rail, in 1888, after the halibut schooner *Oscar and Hattie* came in from off Cape Flattery loaded down to her scuppers. With no refrigerator cars in those days, the cargo had to be iced down, but by the time the train reached Chicago a large share of the shipment had gone bad, and nothing in the world smells worse than rancid halibut, almost bad enough to repulse a square-headed Norwegian. Improved methods produced better results, and by 1895, the traditional Gloucester, Mass., halibut industry was complaining about "stiff competition from the west."

Steamers were introduced to the industry in the early 1890's with such names as the *Iona, Velos* and *Eliza Edwards,* but in 1898, the first vessels designed exclusively for the industry, the *New England* and the *Edith* arrived on the scene. Many ex pelagic sealing schooners, banned by government edict from such pursuits were fitted with engines and became "legitimate" fishing craft.

Cod also became a big demand item, and where powered craft went after other varieties of fish, many of the venerable old lumber schooners replaced by steam-powered craft in the coasting trades, found employment in the cod business and continued to spread their canvas. Many of the old breed of windjammer men, manned them for the annual treks to the Bering Sea, where dorries would fan out and come back with a bonanza of cod to salt down in the schooner holds. Profits remained good enough for ships of sail to keep going up till 1950. Wet eyes watched the curtain come down as the three-masted schooner *C. A. Thayer* made her final voyage to the northland, holding on until after the demise of the larger four-masted *Sophie Christenson.* Their final holdout port was colorful little Poulsbo, on serene Liberty Bay, where for years, crusty Captain J.E. Shields (who once defied the entire Japanese fishing fleet when it invaded Alaska's fishing grounds), and his mild-mannered son, Ed, kept things moving. Their Poulsbo operation was unique, for the little seaport was an ideal location, inasmuch as 90 per cent of its population had remained Norwegian, and annually, Norwegian Independence Day is celebrated. The town was founded in 1882, by, well you might have guessed — a Norwegian named Eliason.

Surprisingly, up through the 1870's the principal means of catching Puget Sound fish commercially was by use of brush weirs, traps and reef nets much as had the

Indians for countless centuries. Fish wheels and gill nets were also used by the early settlers. The purse seine, was initially introduced by the Chinese in 1886. Traps or pound nets, made of webbing or wire netting supported by piling, were often used in estuaries. The fish wheel, however, was a widely used method being composed of a rotary scoop, mounted on a stationary or floating base revolved by the stream, or flow of the tide.

By 1910, the fishing industry in the state had reached $5.5 million in annual value and that didn't take into account the growing oyster industry. Some 3,700 workers were employed, and three years later, there was a record catch or nearly 42 million fish. The value of the processed salmon alone reached a total of more than $14 million, and nearly 16,000 persons were employed in the overall fishing industry. In 1908, Japanese oyster seed was introduced, and in some cases, proved to thrive better in Washington waters than in its native Japan.

In 1939, the state boasted a salmon pack of 727,116 cases; Seattle had also become the leading halibut port of the world with more than 22 million pounds. Since that year many innovations and sophisticated fishing vessels have been introduced to the fishery, and Puget Sound continues to get a large bulk of the catch from North Pacific waters which are sold fresh, canned and processed.

As long as there are fish to catch, man will go after them, whether for business or pleasure. For at least 2,000 years commercial fishing has flourished, for as author A. K. Larssen points out, there was one Simon, known among his fellows as ''The Big Fisherman,'' and to history as ''St. Peter the Rock,'' who operated a small fleet of fishing vessels on the Sea of Galilee.

Towing out to sea — the ship **ABNER COBURN** of Seattle, an old Downeaster, which later engaged in the Alaska salmon canning trade. She was scrapped in 1929.

One of the last of the colorful fleet of three-masted codfish schooners is the **C.A. THAYER** which went to the Bering Sea for many years to bring back her catch in the old style — salted down in her holds. After retirement, the **THAYER** was purchased by the State of California as a floating museum and has been restored to her former splendor as a lumber drougher, having been built in 1895 at Fairhaven, Calif. Her homeport for many years was Poulsbo, on Puget Sound. Photo courtesy Capt. Harold Huycke.

It's anybody's guess, but those rolls of canvas filling the decks of the tug **TRIO,** are probably ships' sails about to be delivered to a sailing vessel somewhere in the harbor. The dock, at the foot of Marion Street, was for many years the home of Sunde & d'Evers Co., ship chandlers. The **TRIO** built at Decatur, Washington in 1911, as a shrimper, later became a Cary-Davis tug.

For many years, the steamers of the Libby, McNeill and Libby fleet took cannery workers north from Seattle to man the Alaska canneries, returning a few months later with the men and valuable cargoes of canned salmon. Prior to the steamers, square-rigged sailing vessels served the purpose. In the above photo, the SS **GENERAL W.C. GORGAS** readies for the voyage. In the lower photo, the MS **LIBBY MAINE** prepares to depart her Seattle pier, as well wishers bid farewell to cannery laborers and management personnel. In the background, is the well known Fisher's Flouring Mill dock, a landmark on the Seattle waterfront down to the present day.

Along the Seattle waterfront, longshoring, a few decades back, was much different than it is today. Upper, the Japanese freighter **ATAGO MARU** discharges bales of silk from the Far East. Lower, The SS **EASTERN GALE** lifts a sling load of canned salmon.

In this faded old photo is a facet of Seattle that few recall. It shows the early home of the Elliott Bay Yacht & Launch Co., looking south from the present Union Oil dock. In more modern times yachts seldom went into Elliott Bay for fear of getting their hull paint dirty. Metro in our day, has made the brine of the waterfront much more acceptable.

The fishing fleet tied up at Salmon Bay bordering Seattle's Lake Washington Ship Canal. The larger vessels, at center of photo, made annual voyages to the Alaska fishing grounds, many at the time, still using sail. Photo was probably taken in the early 1920's.

Cannery ships of the Libby McNeill & Libby fleet at Lake Union head-quarters in Seattle, in the late 1920's. The steamship is the **OTSEGO,** and bark nearest to the camera at right, the **ORIENTAL,** dating from 1874.

Chapter Five
Steamboats Are A'Comin'

Farewell to sail, steam's on the way,
Old things are passed, unhappy day.
                    —JAG

EVOLUTION IN SEA transport has changed more in the past 50 years than in the previous 5,000. The many new types of ship propulsion have become remarkable innovations through the years — steam, diesel, diesel electric, steam turbine, water jet, gas turbine, nuclear — but nothing had such a profound effect on the mind of man as did the initial changeover from sail to steam. For thousands of years countless armadas of ships spread their wings to the winds and not only bridged all the oceans and explored their every corner, but further became the means of world-wide trade. Make no mistake, the traditional did not die easily. It was a hard pill to swallow for the seafarers of the long accepted way, and many refused to bow to the inevitable steamboat with its noise and smut. But, like it or not, the steamer was to become the more dependable mode of water transport, and despite their many flaws in the beginning, the transition had to come. Perhaps the men of sail had somewhat the same feeling as the Puget Sound Indians when their traditional dugouts were crowded out by the superior craft of the early settlers. What would a tiny cedar Indian canoe look like alongside one of today's huge 900 foot containerships, 1,200 foot supertankers, 700 foot roll on/roll off ships, or 600 foot cruise liners? Merely a speck, not even as large as the lifeboat from one of the aforementioned behemoths of the sea would be the dugout.

Coming after the canoe on Puget Sound was the small sailing vessel by which the settlers traveled from one place to another and carried their produce for trade. Then on the scene came the cumbersome side-wheel steamer and the more adequate sternwheeler both of which completely baffled and frightened the poor old Indian, who in essence was like a hitch-hiker sitting on the beach seeking a ride, nobody bothering to pick him up. He was speechless about such innovations in transportation, but not the early Chinese, most of whom were illegally smuggled down from British Columbia to afford cheap labor. Like the Greeks, they had a word for everything, especially the steamers: "No pushee, no pullee, alle same go like helle!"

Initially, Port Townsend was to have been the most important seaport on Puget Sound, and for awhile it was, but fate ruled differently. Most all commerce coming into Admiralty Inlet and Puget Sound called at Port Townsend, strategically located at the entrance to the inland sea. In an earlier chapter we mentioned the first steamer on Puget Sound, Hudson's Bay Company's *Beaver*, and that the first American inland steamer was the *Fairy,* both of which were well known at Port Townsend. When the *Fairy* ended her short life, a new dimension in steamers came to Port Townsend in the form of the iron hulled *Traveler.* Coming up the coast from San Francisco under the experienced hand of Captain J. G. Parker, the vessel was rebuilt at Port Gamble for her new role. Oh, unhappy day, the *Traveler's* longevity was akin to her predecessor, and after only three years she fell victim to a sudden squall off Foulweather Bluff, which claimed the lives of five persons, including her master, Captain Thomas Slater.

One of the most successful of the early Puget Sound steamers was the **ELIZA ANDERSON.** Built at Portland, Oregon in 1859, she made maritime history and also much melody with her famous calliope.

Then came the *Eliza Anderson,* steaming into Puget Sound in a blaze of glory, her big sidewheels destined to stir up billions of gallons of brine in the four decades that lay ahead. On her arrival from the Columbia River, in command of Captain John T. Wright, the locals whooped and hollered as the 140 foot, 280 ton Portland-built craft docked in the spring of 1859. She was one of those "charm" vessels from the start, always dependable and a good bread winner. Of competition, she had none, nor did any complain about the steep rates charged — cattle, $15 a head and all other freight $10. Passengers got socked a whopping $20 from Olympia to Victoria, proportionately less for ports nearer the final destination. For a whole decade, it was the *Eliza* all the way, piling up profits as high as $6,000 per month. Captain Wright, along with his associate, Captain Duncan B. Finch, grew wealthy with his saltwater workhorse, and no Puget Sounder was unfamiliar with the vessel, nor was there hardly a soul who had not peopled her decks at one time or another, nor one who had in mind a sea going career that had not worked as a deckhand or as one of her black gang. Occasionally, a local Indian would even get up enough nerve to ride the "steam kettle."

In later years, as competition arrived in the form of newer and sometimes faster steamers, Captain Wright had little care, for he had piled up a bundle of greenbacks and was able to either buy out his challengers or do it the hard way, by winning out in a rate war. His vessel was loved by all, probably because she was like an old shoe, having been through it all with the early settlers. And then of course, Wright was a pretty regular sort of a guy himself, and no slouch as a PR man. He had installed on the *Eliza* a steam calliope that not only thrilled the kids, but made a pretty good impression on the parents as well. The calliope blared out with Yankee Doodle or John Brown's Body, along with a few other patriotic ditties.

Once, on the Fourth of July, to the vexation of the staid citizens of Victoria, the calliope blared Yankee Doodle for an hour running, while at the Canadian dock. This did not set well with those of British descent and Wright was asked in no uncertain terms to "silence his music maker or shove off." Not desiring to have the local gendarmes tie up his vessel for "disturbing the public," he quietly called for his deckhands to take in the lines, moved the *Eliza* out into the bay and resumed the serenade with all the gusto his musical contraption could generate.

92

Then on the scene came L. M. and E. A. Starr, who purchased the little steamer *Alida* while she was still on the grid at Olympia. After a remodeling at Seattle, she began service from Puget Sound ports to Victoria in the summer of 1870. With old age creeping up on the *Eliza*, the noise in her joints prompted the Wright's to contract for a new deluxe vessel at New York, one that would better fit the needs of a growing Puget Sound populace. The result was the 180 foot sidewheel steamer *Olympia,* which in 1869 made her way around the toe of South America and arrived on the Sound December 7 of the same year to a tumultuous welcome. Highly seaworthy, she boasted a seasoned white oak hull.

Not to be outdone, the Starrs ordered a steamer of comparable size, the 167 foot (178 feet overall) *North Pacific* from a San Francisco yard, and it was obvious to all that competition was building between the Wrights and the Starrs. With public sentiment running high, the inevitable was bound to happen. On June 14, 1871, the *North Pacific* entered the Sound with all her flags proudly flying and before she even reached her first port, hundreds of dollars were already on the line as to which was the faster of the two sidewheelers. Both were evenly matched in size and speed and the respective owners had

sound financial backing. The iron was thrown in the fire on June 29, when Captain Starr offered free rides on his new steed. The rate war was on, but before either side could consider profits on operation a race would have to be run to see which was the "greyhound of Puget Sound waters" and which would have the right to display the broom above her pilot house. Nobody had to wait for long.

Two days later the contestants were at the starting gate at Victoria. It was agreed that they would race across the Strait of Juan De Fuca to Port Townsend, winner take all. Both were well down in the water with passengers and freight, and frantic last minute efforts were made aboard the respective vessels to get every ounce of horsepower from their big steam plants. They backed out into the stream amid deafening roars of excited passengers and whistle blasts, and almost immediately the paddlewheels were churning and the walking beams pumping as fuel was pitched into the boilers to make the big engines heat up like Dante's inferno.

Out into open water, hardly a stone's throw apart, the steamers raced side by side so evenly matched that neither could gain a lead. Shouts and insults were hurled across the watery stretch separating the vessels as the

The pioneer sidewheel steamer **ALIDA** moored at her Seattle dock in the year 1870. Note that budding town, named for the great Indian chief. At the top of the hill is the territorial University of Washington, where today stands the Olympic Hotel. The **ALIDA**, fashioned of Northwest timber at Olympia in 1869, lasted slightly over two decades her tragic end coming at Gig Harbor, when allegedly set afire by flaming debris from a huge forest fire. This photo may have been taken on July 12, 1870 on the occasion of the vessel's inaugural trip from Seattle to Victoria, after having been rebuilt at Seattle for the new service.

Seattle's waterfront probably late 1880's featuring the fine old sidewheel steamer **OLYMPIAN** tied up at the Oregon Improvement Co. dock. She, and her sistership **ALASKAN**, were giant iron-hulled craft that demanded great quantities of fuel to keep their engines operating and walking beams pumping to turn the massive wheels. The **OLYMPIAN** came around the toe of South America to Puget Sound after completion at Wilmington, Delaware in 1883. She was 261 feet long with a beam of 40 feet. This old photo is credited to the pioneer Lardche's Rainier studios.

neck-and-neck competition continued mile after mile, great frothy wakes being trailed astern and thick black smoke pouring from the stacks. To get more speed, tossing all precautions to the wind, combustibles were heaved into the boilers. Never in the annals of Northwest marine history had there been such a contest, and certainly never by two more evenly matched vessels. Finally, the *North Pacific* managed to get just a shade of open water on her rival. The boilers on the respective steamers glowed red, the poppet valves were open wide and the danger of an explosion was all to apparent. A scant three minutes ahead, the *North Pacific* entered Admiralty Inlet, and barely held her lead as she turned into Port Townsend Bay, pushed by her rival all the way to her berth to the exuberant encouragement of her passengers and crew. The *Olympic* pulled in just behind. There was mayhem on the dock, when it was announced the course had been covered in two hours and 41 minutes.

The race was over, but the rivalry continued, both sides cutting rates to the bone to the jubilation of the passengers who could make the trip from Port Townsend to Victoria and return for a mere two-bits. It was a losing game with bankruptcy as the booby prize. Neither would give in. Finally the Starr camp offered to pay the *Olympia's* owners an annual subsidy of $7,500, to exit their craft. The offer was accepted and the Wright steamer was ushered off to San Francisco in July 1871, where a need for such a vessel existed.

Seven years later, after paying out $50,000 in subsidies, the Starr syndicate balked on further payments. This stirred up a beehive and lo and behold, guess what came steaming back to Puget Sound? The errant stranger *Olympia* had come back home to roost. Things began to happen fast, but to prevent a repetition of the earlier standoff both companies entered into another deal whereby the Wrights sold to the Starrs all of their interests on the Sound including the Olympia dock. Then in turn Wright sold the *Olympia* to the Hudson's Bay Company for $75,000. The new owners gave her a facelifting and the new name *Princess Louise*. Even the faithful *Eliza Anderson* which was still plugging around on much less demanding routes was disposed of to new owners.

The *North Pacific* continued for awhile longer as the speed queen of Puget Sound, proving herself once again when the maverick steamer *Dakota* challenged her in a race from Victoria to Port Townsend in 1876, but was left a half mile behind at the finish line. Perhaps the stress and strain on her in'ards became evident a decade later when the *North Pacific* broke a shaft on her walking beam and cylinder, repairs coming to a whooping $30,000. Before the mishap, the Starr camp was still king, discouraging much of the competition on the inland sea by lowering rates between Olympia and Tacoma or Seattle to $2; to Port Townsend to $3.50 and to Victoria to $5, meals 75 cents extra and staterooms $4.

It was indeed a sad day when this exceptional sidewheel steamer reached her final port on July 18, 1903. While operated under the Cary Cook & Co. on the Tacoma-Vancouver B.C. route, she grounded in a pea soup fog off Marrowstone Point, badly damaging her hull. The tug *C. B. Smith* jockeyed in to remove the passengers and crew. High tide swept the point, lifting the stricken steamer free from her perch. Unattended, she drifted seaward toward Whidbey Island, the holes in her hull drinking in barrels of brine. Finally she gave up the ghost and went down in deep water, irretrievably lost.

Like a cat with nine lives, the old *Eliza Anderson* kept on steaming around the Sound. Once she was seized by Collector of Customs Beecher at Port Townsend for illegally transporting alien Chinese immigrants across the border from Canada, a trade that gained considerable impetus in the early times. On another occasion she

suddenly sank at her Seattle dock necessitating a salvage job to get her tired old hull afloat again. After years of neglect, she was resurrected for the Klondike gold rush. Despite her aching timbers she managed to get a load of people and freight as far as Dutch Harbor, Alaska and then quietly drifted onto the rocks and died an agonizing slow death.

In the interim, Puget Sound ports were playing host to a growing number of steamers and sailing vessels of every description. Names like the *Yosemite, Alaskan, Olympian, Idaho, T. J. Potter* and a host of others were on the daily shipping pages of local papers. The *Potter* earned a reputation for herself by virtue of another epic race in which she narrowly defeated the Ballard-built ornate sternwheeler *Bailey Gatzert* on the course between Tacoma and Seattle. Time, 1 hour, 22½ minutes. Then there was the *Vashon, Zephyr, Greyhound, Sehome, Idaho,* the *Flyer,* and oh so many others, all of which were responsible for being the lifeline of the many ports along the shores of Peter Puget's pond.

Seattle to Alki Point for ten cents, aboard the steamer **CAMANO**. That was a pretty good bargain even back then, when Luna Park at Duwamish Head was the fun area. Note the two in the skiff tied up to the bell buoy.

It's been several decades since units of the "Mosquito fleet" called at the old dock at Alki Point with passengers and small parcels of freight. Those were the fun days when the colorful little steamers stopped at legions of docks throughout Puget Sound. Above is seen the steamer **FAIRHAVEN** landing its passengers at Alki, near the place where the founders of Seattle landed aboard the schooner **EXACT** November 13, 1851. Magnolia Bluff, and Queen Anne Hill can be seen in the background across the placid waters of Elliott Bay.

Citizens of Port Townsend long remembered the steamer *J. B Libby,* built at Utsalady on Camano Island in 1862 for Captain S. D. Libby. Initially a sidewheeler, the vessel was converted to a propeller steamer and placed on the Port Townsend-Neah Bay run. Sold to Captain James Morgan, and then in 1889 to Captain H. F. Beecher for $12,000, she entered the Roche Harbor lime trade. En route from San Juan Island to Port Townsend with 500 barrels of lime in her holds, she got caught in the throes of a gale on the Strait of Juan de Fuca, about ten miles from Whidbey Island. Her rudder was dislodged and she rolled and pitched at unprecedented angles, the violent action causing the lime to catch on fire. Captain Frank White tried to run for the nearest shore to beach the steamer, but finally was forced to order abandonment. Fortunately all hands were rescued, and a few days later, the steam schooner *Jeanie,* towed in the gutted hull of the *Libby* —a mass of charred timbers, good only for kindling wood.

The last of the "small fry" sailing schooners to operate on the Port Townsend-Neah Bay and waypoints mail run was the *Winifred,* which for many years did her job and did it well, under nothing but canvas. The steamer *Despatch,* built at Port Madison in 1876, managed two years later to wrest the mail contract away from the "Winnie's" owners. Many bemoaned the changeover, for though the schooner operated at the whims of the wind and was seldom ever on time, she and her skipper, Captain "Billy the Butch," had become a tradition.

Few early day Puget Sound steamers were more accident and mishap prone than the gospel steamer *Evangel.* A member of the clergy, the Reverend J.P. Ludlow, received a calling to take the word of God to the isolated shores of the north Pacific — especially to the Indians, the loggers and the seafaring men who perhaps had never darkened the doorway of a church. To do this he needed a floating conveyance. Having been left some money by a rich uncle, Reverend Ludlow, encouraged others to rally to his cause and sympathetic doners responded, making it possible to sign a contract in Seattle in 1882 for the construction of a suitable steamer.

Though his intentions were highly honorable, the good pastor ran into financial difficulties before the steamer was completed, forcing him to return all of the money that doners had invested, at least that was the general assumption. In turn, he leased his steamer to commercial operator John Leary, the money being used to pay off the debts. As if God frowned on the turnabout, and in all probability he did, the vessel was jinxed from the outset — one mishap after another. She carried the name *Evangel,* but her original mission never came to fruition. Six years later, Ludlow sold his 150 ton wooden hulled steamer to Captain James Morgan for $9,500, who in partnership with Captain Winfield S. Mann intended to rid the vessel once and for all of her problems. But the jinx continued, for in 1890 the *Evangel* collided with the sternwheeler *Skagit Chief* off Five Mile Point, both receiving severe damage.

Nothing was quite so gay as a day in May when the steamer landed at Three Tree Point. Here in the bygones, the steamer **VASHON** pulls into the landing, just southwest of Seattle.

A year later the *Evangel's* boiler exploded at Sehome (Bellingham), taking the lives of three men. In the frequent fogs on the Strait of Juan de Fuca, it was not uncommon for the steamer to run her snout up on low-lying Dungeness Spit, due to the haphazard operation of her skipper, Jim Morgan, who apparently was more concerned with his hand at poker than he was with keeping a proper course. His greatest critic was his partner Win Mann who made no bones about telling the other that his navigation left much to be desired. Then he, Mann, on his turn at being skipper, put the *Evangel* in a most embarrassing position in a heavy fog on Port Townsend Harbor by running under the bowsprit of a tall English square-rigger. There followed a mad scramble aboard the steamer as the well secured bowsprit shaved clean the *Evangel's* mast, wheelhouse and stack, in that order. Her quartermaster, Charley Glasscock (later an Alaska Steamship Co. master), described her appearance as that of "a plucked chicken."

After the pieces were put back together, some suggested that the ill-fated steamer might have been better off to have ended it all right there. And maybe they were right, for a short time after, while crossing the Strait from Lopez Island with a cargo of potatoes, she got caught in a strong cross-sea and running tide which put her over on her beam ends. Spuds began rolling at will from broken gunny sacks in her holds. Caught in irons and held over by excess weight, it was feared she would turn turtle. Captain Morgan ordered every man that could

be spared to get below and right the cargo. For fear of being trapped like rats, the men creeped out of the hold without the knowledge of the skipper who had his hands full elsewhere.

Suddenly the steamer came on to a stretch of calm water and slowly righted herself, Morgan praised his crew for saving the vessel, and on reaching port gave a glowing account of the incident. It became quite a joke, for as it turned out, the "gallant" crew had shifted only two sacks of potatoes before crawling out of the dark chasm to the semi-security of the afterdeck.

The *Evangel* voyaged on into one problem after another. Finally at Port Angeles in 1894, she simply sank to the bottom while at dockside. Morgan eventually got her raised but on paying the salvors found himself without funds to keep her operating. Nobody wanted the floating "Jezabel," except the wreckers, who paid a ridiculous sum at a sheriff's auction to settle accumulated debts.

An so it was that the *Evangel* died.

In the beginning, it was planned that things would go much differently. A little girl dressed in white raiment showered religious tracts upon the scores of people who had gathered below the launching platform, a ceremony designed to take the place of the traditional champagne christening. Old seadogs predicted trouble. While yet on the building ways, 20 feet was added to the vessel's length so that she would be able to carry more cargo; this after Ludlow lost his vision and chartered his life-long

Full house at Colman Dock, mecca of the mosquito fleet before the days of the big auto ferries. At right, is the popular steamer **INDIANAPOLIS.** The vessel under the Colman bell clock is the venerable **CITY OF EVERETT,** her bow to the stern of the KCT steamer **BURTON,** along with several of her counterparts, lined up like dominoes.

dream to John Leary. The latter managed to grab the Alaska mail contract away from the influential Pacific Coast Steamship Company.

It was while the *Evangel* was making her initial voyage to Alaska that the crown sheet of her boiler burned out off Victoria. The Port Discovery mill tug, *S. L. Mastick* towed her to the nearest port, where expensive repairs were undertaken. God had the final say after the on-again off-again clergyman turned his craft over for commercial rather than spiritual purposes. The remainder of the story has already been told. Perhaps countless heathen along the shores of Puget Sound, British Columbia and Alaska were deprived of hearing the gospel because of the maverick steamer, or perhaps we should say, "floating backslider."

A big name in Northwest transportation in the early years was Oregon Railway and Navigation Company, which took over, among other things, the Starr interests and their steamers *North Pacific* and *George E. Starr.* In 1884, they also took delivery of the big sidewheeler *Olympian,* built on the east coast especially for the Puget Sound-Victoria route. Arriving with the typical "big splash," her 32 foot diameter paddlewheels caught the eyes of countless admirers. Shortly, she inaugurated the first round trip schedule from Tacoma to Victoria, and the popularity of the stepped-up service quickly brought

a sistership, the *Alaskan,* to further beef up the operation. Unfortunately, those supersized wheels also demanded super amounts of fuel, and the *Olympain,* though popular with her customers, placed such a financial strain on the owners that they sent her to the Columbia River and later put her on the Alaska run, mostly with the same results. After a short career she ended up in a wrecker's yard.

The *Alaskan,* on the other hand, came to an even more untimely end. While en route to San Francisco in 1889, she encountered a big blow off the Oregon coast. When abreast of Cape Blanco, she foundered taking down with her 31 persons.

A story is told of the *Olympian* on one of her initial trips out of Victoria for Port Townsend. Five Chinese stowaways had hidden themselves inside the paddlewheel housing in the hope they could reach American soil, undetected. Though fully expecting to get wet from the wheel spray, they underestimated the amount of water thrashed about inside the coverings. On reaching Port Townsend, only last gasp moans from the nearly drowned coolies brought about their rescue. After their frightening experience, they were "rewarded" by being sent back to Canada for illegal entry.

Meanwhile the Canadians were becoming highly competitive in water transportation. The steamer *Pre-*

The Lake Washington sternwheel steamer **MERCER** was tantamount to a slow boat to China, but she got her work done and her passengers ranked her with the best, as did her owner, J. L. Anderson. Somebody prominent must have died when this photo was taken as the ensign is at half-mast.

Steamer **H. B. KENNEDY** glides gracefully along on the Seattle-Bremerton route several decades back. This popular vessel performed stellar service, until the advent of the auto ferry, and then underwent a conversion. Her happy crew poses for a photo at dockside.

The new 20 knot steel steamer **TACOMA** was placed on the Seattle-Tacoma run shortly after her completion at Seattle Construction & Drydock Company in 1913. Captain Everett Coffin took over as her master the following year, and remained with the 836 ton, 221 foot long, rakish steamer till she was "finished with engines." Washington's governor Ernest Lister, was present at the launching and his daughter christened the vessel, which was destined to break all records on the run. Challengers quickly fell by the wayside including the steamer **KITSAP II,** of the "white collar" Kitsap fleet. Her pencil thin lines show why her triple expansion 3,750 hp engine was able to beat all competition.

mier made her appearance in 1887 under the Canadian Pacific banner. OR&N's steamer *Victorian,* flying the stars and stripes, tried to outdo the Canadian competition in 1891, but failed. What it was unable to do, fate accomplished, for five years later while on the Port Townsend-Seattle run, the *Premier* locked horns with the SS *Willamette* in a fog off Marrowstone Point, resulting in the loss of four lives and injuries to 20 others. The respective captains had their licenses revoked following a hearing over the matter. The *Premier,* seriously damaged, was towed to port and reconstructed, emerging with the new name, *Charmer,* to erase the unfortunate memory of the previous incident.

About the same time, the Puget Sound and Alaska Steamship Company was formed. Under the management of Captain D. B. Jackson who got OR&N to relinquish its Puget Sound business, the company purchased the sizable passenger steamer *City of Kingston,* originally designed in 1884 for the Hudson River trade. Coming around from New York, via the Straits of Magellan to Port Townsend under Captain Melville Nichols, she arrived to no small amount of fanfare on March 15, 1890. Her pleasing lines, elegant staterooms and outstanding cuisine quickly endeared her to all traveling between Puget Sound ports and Victoria. The 246 foot,

First train to run on tracks into Port Townsend caused quite a stir. The end of the line stopped abruptly in the center of town. Port Townsend's great distance from transcontinental hookups seriously thwarted its progress. Redding's Studio photo.

800 ton *City of Kingston* had stateroom accommodations for 300 and a passenger carrying capacity three times that large. It was indeed a sad occasion just nine years later when the beloved steamer went to the bottom of Tacoma's Harbor after being sliced apart amidships by the ocean steamer *Glenogle*. So severe was the crash that the latter ship had her steel bow section crumpled up clear back to No. 1 hatch. Miraculously, no lives were lost.

Robert Moran, who later immortalized himself as a Seattle shipbuilder, said of the *City of Kingston;* "She was the most satisfactory steamer that ever covered the Puget Sound-Victoria route under the American flag."

Another big event that got considerable news coverage in local newspapers was the launching in May of 1890, of the splendid sternwheel steamer *Bailey Gatzert* from the John J. Holland Shipyard at Ballard. She was built for the Seattle Steam Navigation & Transportation Company, a firm with capital stock of $500,000. One of the finest inland passenger vessels ever turned out on the Sound, she was purchased by the Columbia River and Puget Sound Transportation Company within a year of her completion and placed on the Seattle-Olympia run. She proved to be a real money maker.

In 1891, an organization was formed at Port Townsend by pooling the tugboats of the Puget Sound Commercial Company, the Port Blakely Mill Company,

Among the last of the grand old gentlemen of the era of commercial Puget Sound steamboating were Captain Howell Parker, left and Captain Harry Wilson. Captain Parker last commanded the steamer **VIRGINIA V** and Captain Wilson, the steamer **SIGHTSEER.** Both had brilliant careers aboard many units of the mosquito fleet. They are pictured here before the epic race in 1948 between the **VIRGINIA** and the **SIGHTSEER** in which the former narrowly nudged out the latter on Elliott Bay. Both of these fine maritime men have since passed away.

Washington Mill Company and the Tacoma Mill Company. Its purpose was to end the dog-eat-dog competition of racing out to meet ocean going ships, mainly tall sailing vessels, to bargain over towing costs — "Tug boat Annie style." Such practices occurred all the way from Cape Flattery to Admiralty Inlet, and occasionally, hardnosed sailing ship skippers, who felt the towing charges excessive would sail their cumbersome commands right up to dockside, providing the breeze cooperated. Thus the Puget Sound Tug Boat Company was formed.

Big steam tugs with names like *Wanderer, Richard Holyoke, Tyee, Tacoma, Goliah, Sea Lion, Magic, Bahada* and *Wyaddah* handled the chores with cooperative dependability without cutthroat tactics. Initially headquartered at Port Townsend, the firm later moved to Seattle to handle the growing amount of ship assistance work from a more central location. Then too, the long tows needed by sailing vessels were not so numerous with the gradual changeover to steam powered ocean ships.

Several new inland sea steamer operations opened in the decade of the 1890's. The Straits Steamship Company was formed under the guidance of L. Hastings, operating the colorful little steamers *Majestic, Lydia Thompson, Garland* and *Hermosa*. Another promising firm was the La Conner Trading & Transportation Company. It was founded by Captain Joshua Green, who went onto maritime and banking fame, finally succumbing at Seattle in 1975 at age 105. Then there was Captain L. B. Hastings who ran the steamer *Dauntless* on the Port Townsend-Port Hadlock-Fort Casey route, carrying passengers, freight and mail, and also operating a fleet of tugs such as the *Enterprise, Wildwood, Edna* and *Virginia*.

On the scene came a company in 1895 that was to last for six decades. Captain Charles Peabody, joined forces with Captain George Roberts, Walter Oakes and George Lent to form the Alaska Steamship Company. Starting out as a one boat operation, the little steamer *Willapa*, which began life as a bar tug, competed against the big and powerful Pacific Coast Steamship Company, which headquartered in San Francisco. Even after being lengthened, she only stretched out to 136 feet, but was able to pack in a fair crowd of passengers as well as cargo. Though her record showed she was built as the Columbia River bar tug *General Miles* at Astoria in 1881, it was said that parts of her hull came from a vessel which was started in 1879. A decade later she capsized on Coos Bay bar, was pulled ashore, and taken to Portland. There she was lengthened and renamed *Willapa*, for operation between Puget Sound and British Columbia ports under Captain H. F. Beecher, former collector of customs for Puget Sound. Beecher sold her to the "new" Alaska Steamship Company in 1895, and the timing for the firm was perfect, for within two years, gold was discovered in the Klondike. Alaska Steam had the ships and would travel. And travel they did. Every ship of the company profited, and continued to do so for decades afterward, shoving aside the competition right up till recent times when economics ended its long domination over Alaska commerce.

Back at the turn of the century, Peabody diverted the smallest steamer of the fleet, the *Rosalie,* to local Puget Sound service, and in 1902 purchased the Thompson Steamboat Company which then owned the steamers

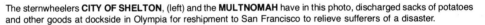

The sternwheelers **CITY OF SHELTON**, (left) and the **MULTNOMAH** have in this photo, discharged sacks of potatoes and other goods at dockside in Olympia for reshipment to San Francisco to relieve sufferers of a disaster.

The port of Shelton as it appeared in 1907. The little sternwheel steamer is the **IRENE**, which ran for many years between south Sound ports. Note the fancy horse drawn carriage being pulled uptown.

Lydia Thompson, Prosper, Majestic, Alice Gertrude and *Garland.* Then Joshua Green arranged a stock deal whereby Peabody would purchase his LaConner Trading & Transportation Company thus adding that fleet consisting of the *Utopia, Fairhaven, George E. Starr, State of Washington, T, W. Lake, Rapid Transit, Inland Flyer* and *Port Orchard.* By 1903, the company, largest of its kind on Puget Sound, was operating as the Puget Sound Navigation Company, with the trade name, "Black Ball Line." The name was by virtue of Peabody being lineal descendent of the old Maine family that once operated the famous Black Ball clipper fleet on the Atlantic. The new company was to operate for more than a half century, son, Captain Alex taking over from his father. Through the years the fleet grew and flourished with such well known steamers as the *Chippewa, Iroquois, Sioux, Potlatch, Flyer, Indianapolis, Waialeale, Sol Duc* and many more, including the most famous of all, the *Tacoma,* which set a new speed record on the Seattle-Tacoma run by doing better than 20 knots following her completion in 1913. For most of her career she was under the capable skipper, Captain Everett B. Coffin.

The Black Ball fleet had a competitor in the Kitsap County Transportation Company with its fleet of white-collared mosquito steamers. There was also the "Navy Yard Route" featuring the *H. B. Kennedy,* and later the passenger steamer *Commander,* (ex General Frisbie) which gave Black Ball a good run for its money. Then there was the West Pass Transportation Company with its series of *Virginia's* serving the ports along the west side of Vashon Island and other south sound portals. Like busy bees, at quitting time each day, the steamers would

dart in and out of Elliott Bay, concentrating on the Colman Dock where passengers boarded their respective vessels for just about every port on Puget Sound. Probably, it was the most colorful period ever in the workaday world of water transportation out of Seattle.

By the time the transition from passenger steamers to automobile ferries had come about, Black Ball Line had bought out most of the competition and were operating a growing fleet of ferryboats. Some of the smaller ports lost out with the demise of the passenger steamers, fading into nothingness, or settling for a role of a quiet little village. Most of the units of the mosquito fleet passed into oblivion, except for a few of the largest which underwent conversion to auto ferries. As time and demand continued, the pioneer ferries fell by the wayside and bigger more commodious ferries were constructed. One of the great "publicity boats" of the Black Ball fleet was the nation's first streamlined ferry, the *Kalakala,* (Flying Bird) resurrected in 1935 from the gutted hull of a former San Francisco ferryboat. The all-silver craft attracted attention the world over. Her major problem was vibration. Her shakedown cruise proved to be exactly that — she shook out most of her windows and portlights. Alterations helped solve much of the problem. The second difficulty was in the pronunciation of her Indian name by the many tourists who "insisted" on riding her on the Seattle-Bremerton run. Unable to pronounce *Kalakala,* she became known to many as "Cococola."

When the San Francisco Bay bridges were opened, ending an almost legendary era of California water transportation, Puget Sound Navigation managed to buy up a generous portion of the surplus ferries for a song, and these along with the other company vessels performed

The funny little steamer **WILLIE** alongside the historic Percival's Dock in Olympia. The **WILLIE** played a leading role in the maritime history of Shelton, operating as she did between that port and Olympia from 1886 till 1900, when passengers and freight moved mostly by water. She was owned by Lan and Lafe Willey, sons of Sam Willey, early settler and logger. (Courtesy Bill Somers)

Diesel ferry **BALLARD**, formerly the ferry **LIBERTY**, for several years operated on the Ballard-Port Ludlow route, beginning in the early 1930's.

Change in Schedule

Kingston-Port Ludlow Route
SCHEDULE EFFECTIVE
NOV. 15, 1927

LEAVE SEATTLE
PIER 3

Daily · - · 3:00 p.m.
Saturday · 1:30 p.m.
Sunday, 9 a.m. & 6:30 p.m.

FOR

Newelhurst   Kingston
Appletree   Hansville
Eglon   Port Ludlow
and Port Gamble

STEAMERS
Monticello, Mohawk
or Narada

stellar service during the World War II era, especially on the busy Seattle-Bremerton route.

Increasing demands, high costs of operation, and agitation by the State against higher fares, prompted Peabody to sell his fleet in 1951 to the State of Washington for $5 million. He in turn, started a new Black Ball Line in British Columbia which he operated until 1961, and then sold out to the British Columbia government for a second handsome profit. both fleets have since been completely modernized, with many ''superferries'' to meet the ever-increasing demands of the public on wheels, connecting with the endless gray-ribboned highways.

An institution that had its meager beginnings on the Tacoma waterfront is the Foss Launch & Tug Company. Founded as a small boat rental service in the 1880's, catering mostly to sailing ships anchoring in Commencement Bay, it grew into the largest towing firm in the Pacific Northwest. Remaining as a family operation until recent times, the controlling interest has since been purchased by the huge Dillingham enterprise of Honolulu. The Foss name has been retained. Principal competition through the years has been from the Puget Sound Tug & Barge Company, a long time Seattle firm that in recent times was purchased by the Crowley interests of San Francisco. It has since grown into one of the world's largest towing aggregations, boasting the familiar Red Stack symbol and international name, ''Crowley Maritime.''

When Andrew and Thea Foss founded the Foss firm, they began with personal service via rowing skiffs. They then graduated to naptha launches and gas launches, and finally branched out into the tug and barge field to fill a growing need. The management fell to the three Foss sons, Henry, Wedell and Arthur, who lived up to the company motto in every sense of the word, and that word was, ''Always Ready.''

In 1927, the little steamers **MONTICELLO, MOHAWK** and **NARADA** made regular calls at Kingston, Port Ludlow, and all of the little North Kitsap Peninsula whistlestops. Then came the automobile ferries and the whole scene changed, many of the little ports being lopped off the schedule. The old schedule card is reproduced here.

The steamer **NARADA** of the Port Ludlow-Kingston Transportation Company, with the alias's of **TYPHOON** and **VIRGINIA III,** makes her regular stop at Eglon in the late 1920's. The **NARADA** was built at Tacoma in 1910. Note the condition of the planking on the dock. Looks like an invitation to a lawsuit. The steamer schedule card for the route is seen below.

The automobile ferry **NISQUALLY,** one of the former San Francisco Bay shuttlers, is pictured here landing at Port Ludlow in the summer of 1946. The ferry route no longer exists.

APPROXIMATE SCHEDULE
TO SEATTLE

FROM	WEEK	SATURDAY	SUNDAY
ort Gamble	5:40 a.m.		
ort Ludlow	6:30 a.m.	5:00 p.m.	3:00 p.m.
ansville	7:00 a.m.		3:40 p.m.
:lon	7:30 a.m.		4:00 p.m.
ingston	8:00 a.m.	6:30 p.m.	4:45 p.m.
ewelhurst	8:15 a.m.		4:50 p.m.

Steamer **HYAK,** one of the mainstays of the Kitsap County Transportation Company in the mosquito fleet days, is seen at dockside at Port Madison, on Bainbridge Island. Port Madison was once the site of a flourishing lumber mill and was named by the Wilkes Expedition in 1841, for President Madison.

Departing the little port of Brinnon on Hood Canal, the steamer **PERDITA** gets up a head of steam. Her career was unfortunately, short, beginning at Seattle in 1903 and ending only eight years later, when she caught fire off Port Ludlow while traveling at full speed ahead. With the fire having originated in the engine room, the vessel could not be stopped. Captain A.N. McAlpine, ordered the stateroom doors torn off and all floatable material dumped overboard, followed in quick sucession by passengers and crewmen who hung on until rescued by two launches. The **PERDITA** was totally gutted. Black Ball was running her on the Seattle-Port Townsend and wayport route.

Proud captain and crew of the steamer **HYAK,** say "cheese" for the cameraman, when the rakish little steamer was on the cross Sound route (Kitsap County Transportation Co.) from Seattle to Poulsbo and Bainbridge waypoints. The vessel was built in 1909 at Portland, Oregon.

Steamer **ROSALIE,** lower photo, at picturesque Orcas, on Orcas Island in the fantastic San Juan Islands. The sleepy little port has changed little through the years since these photos were taken. The **ROSALIE** was built at Alameda in 1893, one of the veterans of the Puget Sound Navigation Company. Upper photo shows another steamer leaving the port, in a hillside view.

Orcas, as it appeared in 1946, as the ferryboat **VASHON** prepares to land stern first to pick up vehicles seen on the road above the dock shed.

Activity on the Everett docks in the early years of this century. The steam tug **GRACE THURSTON** is in the foreground. The large sternwheeler at the outer side of the dock, is the **CAPITAL CITY.**

The G. W. L. Allen Wharf at Samish Island, (one of the San Juan group) due north of Whidbey Island. The steamer coming in for a landing is probably the venerable old sternwheeler **STATE OF WASHINGTON.** Shallow water necessitated the lengthy pier.

A vintage photo of the steamer **QUICKSTEP,** taken well before the turn of the century at the Newcastle Landing on Lake Washington. According to Captain Bob Matson, marine historian for Lake Washington water transportation, Captain John L. Anderson is in the wheelhouse; his aunt Emelia on the dock, and Anderson's father in the carriage. The **QUICKSTEP** came up to the Sound from the Columbia River in 1883, and after service on the lake, was destroyed by fire.

Steamer **FORTUNA** at the East Seattle landing on Lake Washington, about 1910. Launch **QUEEN** , is at right. Courtesy Capt. Bob Matson.

Collision course! Where's the Coast Guard? It really isn't quite as bad as it appears. The Canadian Pacific steamer **PRINCESS ADELAIDE** is seen backing away from her Seattle pier, as the steamer **INDIANAPOLIS** gathers speed to cross her bow. To the left, is the coastwise passenger liner **GOVERNOR** which met her waterloo off Point Wilson, near Port Townsend in 1921.

Marysville was only a whistlestop in 1885 as the sternwheeler **MUNROE** tied up to take on slabwood for fuel. Marysville dates back to 1877, when James P. Comeford, established a trading post on Ebey Slough. Nearby the city of Marysville is the Tulalip Indian Reservation.

Down through the years the waters of Puget Sound have played host to a wide variety of odd vessels and colorful characters, but perhaps none capped "Captain" Horton's palace, a strange barge-like craft which he called the **GALLERY.** It was rigged with a single squaresail and defied the viewer to tell whether she was going ahead or astern. Serving as a home and photo workshop, Horton was in no hurry to go anyplace. In the lower photo, he is seen coming aboard after shooting enough game to last him through the winter. Despite the heavy snowfall, his palace looks pretty snug. The extreme shallow-draft of the craft permitted her to go into very shallow water.

Though Victoria, B.C. is not part of Puget Sound, it has been synonymous with the maritime activities of Puget Sound from the beginning. Here, a few decades back, is pictured the colorful Canadian Pacific Princess fleet. One of the oldest units is the SS **CHARMER**, center left.

The Gilkey Bros. towing fleet of Anacortes which got rolling about 1909, steadily built up in size to one of the more formidable on the Sound in earlier years. Here most of their tugs are pictured at the Anacortes headquarters. A Japanese freighter is at the port pier loading lumber. Anacortes, on Fidalgo Island, is a lumber, fishing, and today an oil discharge port. Whaling ship skippers often careened their ships on the island more than a century ago to scrape off accumulated sea growth, mostly at Squaw Harbor (now Ship Harbor). Originally named Magic City, when founded about 1860, the place eventually became Anacortes to honor Anna Curtis, wife of Amos Bowman, an early settler.

"Fly on the Flyer," was the motto for this fleet passenger steamer of the "Flyer Route" between Seattle and Tacoma. Seen here at the latter port, this swift vessel broke several Puget Sound speed records under Captain U. B. Scott's White Collar Line and also under Black Ball, from 1891, when built at Portland, Oregon until her demise in 1929. One of her greatest feats was besting the newer and more commodious **INDIANAPOLIS** in a race between Tacoma and Seattle in the summer of 1910. Her master for many years was genial and colorful Captain Everett B. Coffin. The **TACOMA** made the run between the two ports in one hour and 25 minutes. Steamer **FLEETWOOD** is at her stern.

Genial veteran of Puget Sound waterways was "Cap" Smiley, longtime master of the sternwheeler **GLEANER.** He is seen here at the helm of his vessel. Photo courtesy Phil Shively.

This was a business as usual scene at the Port Blakely Mill Co. in the early days. In the foreground is the bulky sidewheel tug **FAVORITE,** which came up from San Francisco to do towing work for the mill company. Dating from 1868, the old craft lasted till 1919 when she was broken up at Seattle. The steel-hulled ship **ASTER** (white hull) is at dockside.

The venerable old sternwheel steamer **GLEANER** at Anacortes, built at Stanwood in 1907 for the Skagit River Navigation Company of Mt. Vernon.   The vessel was wrecked near Bald Island, on the Skagit, in 1940. Her crew is seen in lower photo, probably about 1910.

In the early 1920's, the 56 foot ferryboat **CITY OF EDMONDS**, built at Clinton for the Edmonds-Kingston ferry run. Note those fancy vehicles on that "super" car slip.

This is believed to be the Snohomish waterfront in about 1892, with the river steamers **MAY QUEEN, MABLE** and another unidentified, at the dock.

Metamorphosis: This is the before and after of the same vessel. Above she is the Key System's San Francisco Bay ferry **PERALTA,** which in 1927 was gutted by fire, leaving only a burned out hulk. Below she emerges as the world's first streamlined ferry, the **KALAKALA,** turned out by the Lake Washington Shipyard in 1935 for service between Seattle and Bremerton. The 18 knot, silver-painted motor vessel gained world-wide attention under the Black Ball banner.

The old and the new. The world's first streamlined ferry, the **KALAKALA**, built from the gutted hull of a San Francisco ferry in 1935, glides along opposite one of the ex-perennials of Puget Sound, the fine old ferryboat **CHIPPEWA**. The latter was built on the Great Lakes at the turn of the century and put in six decades of service, mostly on the Seattle-Bremerton run. Originally, she was a passenger steamer and with the change of the era was converted to an automobile ferry. The **KALAKALA** also outlived her usefulness as a ferry, being sold to Alaska fishing interests. Both vessels served as prime units of the Puget Sound Navigation Co. (Black Ball) and also with the Washington State Ferry System. Photo taken August 30, 1949.

Black Ball Line's popular steamer **INDIANAPOLIS** at the Tacoma Municipal Dock in days of yore.

Parley in the wheelhouse, of the newly constructed sternwheel steamer **JULIA B.**, an 835 ton vessel, built by the yard of Cook & Lake in Ballard in 1908, specially for the Yukon Transportation Company. She and two barges were built for Yukon River operation and towed north by the steamer **A. G. LINDSAY.** Alongside the **JULIA B.** is the tug **CELTIC.**

Built at Port Blakely in 1889, as a tug for the mill firm operation, the **SARAH M. RENTON**, 137 tons, was later converted for passenger and freight operation on the Port Blakely-Seattle run. She was replaced by the more adequate steamers **MONTICELLO** and **ADVANCE**, taken over by the Port Blakely Mill Company from the Moe Brothers. The **RENTON**, with her steeple compound engine, became the Canadian tug **ERIN**. She is pictured here before the turn of the century inbound to Port Blakely Harbor. In the background, just off her stern, is Blakely Rocks.

All set for a Lake Whatcom sternwheel steam cruise aboard the **CORA BLAKE**, May 1, 1904. This funny little craft, originally the **MIKE ANDERSON,** was later named **BRIED,** and as such burned on the lake, near Geneva.

The only way to go — about 1900 — the little 60 foot propeller steamer **ACME** glides up the peaceful Sammamish Slough to Bothell. Built on Lake Washington in 1899, she operated between Leschi and Madison Park and on up to Bothell. N. C. Peterson was her owner-skipper.

114

"We'll put you off anywhere along the line," was the boast of the little steamer **CITY OF BOTHELL** — Bothell, Kenmore, Lake Forest Park, Pontiac, all the whistlestops along the Sammamish River, and north Lake Washington.

Some gayly dressed passengers prepare to board the steamer **FLYER,** in the early years of this century.

Hey! those belles of yesteryear were pretty good looking! This is the launching party for the steamer **SIOUX,** a crack new steel-hulled vessel, launched in December 1910 at the Seattle Construction & Drydock Co. Puget Sound Navigation Company placed their new acquisition on the Seattle-Irondale-Port Townsend run. The lady in the white dress was the sponsor.

Moored at the face of the Ainsworth & Dunn Wharf in Seattle is the venerable sidewheel steamer **GEORGE E. STARR,** which made Puget Sound maritime history.

Two full houses at Tacoma. Above is seen the Municipal Dock, where a host of Sound steamers, mostly of the Black Ball fleet take on passengers for various destinations. The largest is the steamer **INDIANAPOLIS,** built in 1904, and for many years a stalwart carrier on the Tacoma-Seattle run. Below, is a line up of "mosquito" fleet steamers that served Puget Sound ports and whistlestops. The small motor schooner is probably the **O. D. AHLER,** and the first of the steamers in the line up, the sternwheeler **CLARA BROWN.** View is from the 11th Street Bridge.

As it must to every man, so to every ship — death. The proud sidewheel steamer **NORTH PACIFIC**, fast, commodious and popular, from the time she came to Puget Sound in 1871 to her untimely passing in 1903. Built for E.A. and L.M. Starr, the walking beam steamer won out in a classic race with the equally splendid **OLYMPIA**, within weeks after arrival. The contest was run from Victoria to Port Townsend and wasn't far from being a photo finish. Owned by Finch and Wright, the **NORTH PACIFIC** was sold to OR&N in 1881 and stranded off Marrowstone Point in the fog on July 18, 1903. Drifting off the beach into deep water, she plunged to her grave. The historic steamer went down shortly after the lower photo was taken, a Rothschild launch standing by.

Chapter Six
Waterfront Characters, Haunts and Strange Events

Everyone is as God made him,
and often a great deal worse.
                            —Cervantes

WITH FEW EXCEPTIONS the early waterfronts of Puget Sound ports were rough, tough places, not fit for the innocent to tread by nightfall. Akin in most respects to San Francisco's Barbary Coast, they were the inhabitants of some of the scum of the earth, hardened individuals who preyed upon unsuspecting sailors. Runners, prostitutes, brawlers, and toughs gathered in the smoke-filled waterfront saloons and dives, to perform their satanic chores. Under the long bowsprits of sailing vessels at dockside which cast dark shadows under the dim lantern lights, a drama of sinful pursuit went merrily on each night. Worm-eaten piling held up the old wharves, piled high with stacks of lumber, hay, bricks and miscellaneous cargo, and men brawled in the muddy streets as melodian music wafted out from the "gin mills." Rats scurried freely about in dank cellars and across wooden floors; under-nourished mongrel dogs whelped in front of false front buildings and the rancid smell of hash houses and Oriental incense filled the nostrils.

The disciplined mill towns, that had iron clad potentates of the New England brand, were often invaded by the free living element, but if the boss man controlled the payroll, he usually controlled the populace, and the locals would rally to his cause in running the renegades out of town, and back to the more tolerant ports.

There were many well known early day waterfront characters. One that gained considerable prominence haunted the Port Townsend waterfront — not the usual brand of character. His name was Harry L. Sutton and he suffered from a "Dr. Jeckyl and Mr. Hyde" personality. Unlike many of his villanous-appearing counterparts, Sutton came from a prominent shipping family in Boston, was well educated, handsome and almost effeminate in his mannerisms. On arriving at Port Townsend in 1862, he might have been mistaken for a clergyman rather than a hardened criminal. Looks, however, are often deceiving and as the old saying goes, "you can't judge a book by its cover." Hardly out of his boyhood, he had killed two men, who allegedly attacked him while on one of his father's wharves in the dark of night. His parents had paid a large sum of money to keep him out of jail and in turn arranged for a berth on one of the family clipper ships headed for California. In a quest for paydirt in the Cariboo rush, he grew tough as nails but on having only limited success, worked his way down Puget Sound way settling in Port Townsend. For a period he tried to turn into a respectable business man and showing considerable ability worked his way up to the editorship of the *Port Townsend Register,* the local news sheet. Still later he helped establish the *Port Townsend Message.* Going back to his East Coast haunts in 1869 he returned with new presses and equipment for erecting one of the finest publishing setups on Puget Sound. While fast becoming a fearless, crusading editor for *The Message,* suddenly the economy turned sour in the year 1871, and Sutton ran short of money. When facing near bankruptcy, almost overnight he reverted to his former role, becoming mean and ruthless. His noble manner and good looks disappeared and he pursued diverse ventures. Opening a "hellhole" on Union dock, named Blue Light, he gathered about him the most unsavory characters he could find, men who specialized in vice and corruption.

On the scene came a Puget Sound pilot by the name of Charles W. Howard, a short, stocky individual and former pugilist. A one-time friend of Sutton, the two had become the bitterest of enemies even to the point where Sutton had threatened to shoot him on sight. Howard in turn had vowed "to beat the pulp" out of the other. The long awaited showdown came about in the spring of 1877, when one afternoon after bringing a sailing vessel into the bay, Howard started toward Sutton's infamous establishment. Though the pilot's friends had cautioned him not to darken its doors, he only clenched his fist and laughed off the warning. Sutton saw him coming and stood at the entrance, gun in hand.

"Take one step more," threatened the Blue Light's owner, "and I'll fire!"

The fearless pilot sneered as he entered the swinging doors.

Immediately, Sutton opened up, one of the bullets striking Howard in the chest. Falling to one knee, the pilot gasped for breath;

"That's enough, Harry," he uttered, "Don't shoot me again!"

The saloon proprietor showed no mercy and in an impassioned rage fired several more shots, the patrons of the bar scattering in all directions. The writhing body at last lay lifeless on the wooden floor, blood flowing freely from numerous wounds.

Reloading his revolver, Sutton darted up the narrow streets and shadowed alleys where some of his nefarious associates hid him from the authorities. After it grew

dark, he was secreted out of the harbor in a small boat and sailed up the Strait to Port Angeles. There he hid out until an alert sheriff named Ben Miller, and his deputy tracked him down, affording him the choice of surrendering or being shot. Settling for the former, Sutton came out of his hiding place hands above his head and was escorted back to Port Townsend under heavy guard.

Trial was held in the fall of 1877 and Sutton was found guilty. Perhaps the judge was bribed, but the accused got off with a light sentence of five years. Now there sometimes prevails a loyalty even among men of evil pursuits, and Sutton's many friends rallied to his cause, almost to the place of inconceivability. They got permission to furnish his ground floor cell with rugs and furniture. They had flowers brought in to brighten up the dingy spot and often provided him with gourmet foods and reading material. The tolerant jailhouse administration was to regret its leniency, for on one of his morning checks, the jailer found Harry's cell empty. The prisoner had escaped by tunneling under the foundation, the hole in the floor of his cell covered by a rug and table. With Sutton had gone three fellow prisoners. An immediate manhunt rounded up all but our infamous hero, who on paying blood money, managed refuge aboard a ship sailing for California. All that is known of him thereafter is his rumored death in a shootout with an angered Arizona cowboy. As the Good Book says, "He who lives by the sword, dies by the sword!"

One of the well known characters on the Port Townsend waterfront was Kanaka Jack, a full-blooded Hawaiian whose actual name was Nuheana, his father having allegedly been a servant to King Kamehameha. He like many of his race, had gone off to sea at a young age becoming a good sailor, and a hard worker, but while yet wet behind the ears, having been introduced to liquor.

Everett Harbor in the halcyon days, as a group of western-dressed Indians paddle their canoe past the sternwheeler **CAPITAL CITY**. The port of Everett grew into a large lumbering, pulp, and paper exporter, and a distribution point for agricultural products and fish. It is the county seat of Snohomish County.

Indian canoes were still very much in use by the Puget Sound natives long after the white man introduced many of his innovations in water travel.

A handsome array of Lake Washington steamers of the J. L. Anderson fleet are pictured at Leschi Dock on Lake Washington, from where they fanned out to destinations throughout the lake. The two, center left, are the **CYRENE** and **XANTHUS**; in the background the little **MERCER** and in the foreground the launch **RAMONA**.

Anybody for a canoe ride? What better way to spend a lazy Sunday afternoon. This is the old Leschi Boat House, long a landmark on Lake Washington.

Initially engaged as a hand aboard a sugar packet, he sometime later jumped ship on Puget Sound. In one of his sober moments, Jack landed a job in a local cracker company and did well as long as he could resist the "spirits." But, alas, his fleshly weakness prevailed, and while under the influence he got his hands badly mangled in the factory machinery. More bad luck. Shortly after his unfortunate accident he suffered a paralytic stroke. With no funds, his lot worsened, and a slow recovery left him badly deformed with almost useless hands and ex-

treme difficulty in walking about. Like a mongrel dog, he wandered along the waterfront seeking a crust of bread or a swig of liquor. He was scorned and ridiculed, the butt of jest and buffoonery. Among those who took pity on the pathetic Hawaiian was a Mrs. Myra West who had come to Port Townsend from the Hawaiian Islands. She learned of the plight of Kanaka Jack, and on her return to Honolulu contacted authorities. The "aloha spirit" immediately surfaced especially when it concerned a misguided native son, and the Hawaiian vice counsel dis-

John L. Anderson, became "Mr. Steamboat" of Lake Washington from the turn of the century. He not only ran his own shipyard at Houghton but also the Anderson Steamboat Company, headquartered at Leschi Park, gaining a virtual monopoly on lake operations, in the days before any thought of floating bridges. This is the way things looked many decades ago. Courtesy Capt. Bob Matson

Hey! poosh her der Tony. Quit looking at the cameraman! Who's that lazy guy inside just going along for the ride? The vehicle is a shiny Detroit Electric. Courtesy Jack Dillon.

Colorful Roche Harbor on historic San Juan Island, today is the location of a resort built into the original lime town, with all the old structures still standing as they did when the town was operated by the Roche Harbor Lime and Cement Company. Though the plant, founded by John S. McMillan, has not produced for many years, it is surrounded by one of the most picturesque settings in all the greater Puget Sound Country. A pastorial air pervades, the fragrant gardens and the vine-covered balconied De Haro Hotel, where President Teddy Roosevelt once slept. McMillan opened the lime quarries in the 1880's and built the lime plant and company town. The old sailing vessel is the **ROCHE HARBOR LIME TRANSPORT** once used for barging and storage. She was formerly the Scotch built square-rigger **LA ESCO-CESA,** (Scottish lady) later becoming the **STAR OF CHILE,** making many fine passages from the date of her completion at Dundee in 1868. The firm purchased the vessel in 1926. During World War II she went back to sea for a period, under sail.

The Winslow ferry dock in the 1930's, with popular steamer engineer E. L. Franks directing traffic.

patched money to Judge James G. Swan who saw to it that Jack got passage back to his native home. Swan, a recognized historian, author and pioneer, understood the situation from his sometimes frustrating work in getting local Indians proper treatment. He saw to it personally that Kanaka Jack was put aboard the bark *Hope,* placing him under the eye of the ship's master, Captain D. B. P. Penhallow, who himself had been born in Honolulu.

When the *Hope* arrived at the Hawaiian port, the pathetic passenger was placed in Queen's Hospital where he found care and concern, but no more opportunity to pursue his insatiable appetite for liquor. There he lived out his days in peace, never missing an opportunity to ask visitors about the Port Townsend waterfront and the

many seafaring men with whom he had had contact through the years.

One of the most colorful and daring of the early seafaring pioneers on Puget Sound was the redoubtable Captain Jimmy Jones, a Welshman who had emigrated to California in 1849. Shipping aboard the Hudson's Bay vessel *Cadboro* for Victoria B. C., he came to Puget Sound country in 1854 and managed to make enough money to finance the building of the schooner *Emily Parker.* Desiring like many others to fatten his purse during the Fraser River gold strike, Jones took his ship north into Canadian waters where it unfortunately caught on fire and burned to the water's edge. Undaunted by his bad fortune, Jones immediately built the schooner

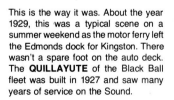

This is the way it was. About the year 1929, this was a typical scene on a summer weekend as the motor ferry left the Edmonds dock for Kingston. There wasn't a spare foot on the auto deck. The **QUILLAYUTE** of the Black Ball fleet was built in 1927 and saw many years of service on the Sound.

QUILLAYUTE

Caroline and operated her between Victoria and Nanaimo. After selling her at a good profit, he constructed the commodious 95 foot schooner *Jenny Jones* at Port Townsend with the aid of Franklin Sherman. Into his splendid creation he placed a small steam engine, which perhaps made her Puget Sound's initial steam schooner. While operating between the Columbia River, B. C. ports and Puget Sound, the schooner had the misfortune of scraping over treacherous Clatsop Spit, narrowly escaping destruction at a spot where just a few years earlier (May 10, 1861) the British schooner *Woodpecker* had met her doom.

After buying out his partner in 1865, Jones began an epic adventure unique in Puget Sound maritime history. While at Victoria, he got involved in financial difficulties and ended up in the local calaboose. His first officer then took the *Jenny Jones* back across the Strait to keep her from being impounded. Meanwhile, waterfront friends came to Jones' assistance. Master-minding an escape, they dressed him up like a woman so as to elude detection, and then arranged passage for the masculine ''lady,'' back to Puget Sound. None was the wiser, in fact, with a clean shaven face, the impersonator managed a few smiles and winks from traveling gentlemen.

After his arrival, Jones learned that his beloved vessel was in the hands of the U.S. marshal at Olympia. Creditors were demanding her sale to pay accumulated debts. When plans were made to send the *Jenny Jones* to Seattle to be auctioned off by the marshal, Jones boarded

This stogy smokin' ship's officer seen aboard the steamer **KULSHAN** back in the good ol' 1920's went on to become recognized Puget Sound pilot, Captain Floyd Smith, who at this writing is still going strong.

her as a passenger. En route, the craft tied up at the Steilacoom dock for the night. The marshal, preferring the comfort of an uptown hotel to the hard bunks aboard the schooner, left her unguarded. Jones daringly seized the opportunity to take command once again, despite the fact, that his action would make him ''the most wanted man'' on both sides of the border. Legally he could not move his ship in either direction, and with only enough fuel for a 40 mile run and supplies consisting of two pounds of sugar, one sack of flour and a pound of tea, he cast off the lines in the still of the night and drifted silently away from the dock. When well out in the stream

Things got a little hectic in 1921, at the East Sound dock on Orcas Island. Picture a summer day as the steamer **SIOUX** tries to get the spring line to the dock. The unusual looking craft on the left is the gas powered passenger boat **YANKEE DOODLE,** which at the moment appears to have priority attention.

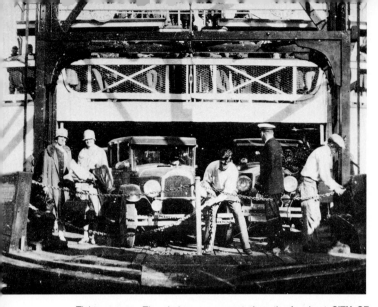

Tight squeeze. The chains are connected as the ferryboat **CITY OF ANGELES**, pulls away from the dock at Lopez, on Lopez Island in the San Juans in the 1920's. It was mighty frustrating when one's car was left waiting at the dock.

Left high and dry among the barnacled piling, the motor freight boat **CHIMACUM** of the Puget Sound Freight Lines is pictured near Luna Park, West Seattle. Aboard were 5,000 crates of choice strawberries, bound from Langley, Whidbey Island to the National Fruit Canning Co. in West Seattle. The vessel was holed, tide flowing in and out of her hull, ruining the entire cargo. She was eventually patched and repaired. The fellow at the left, appears to be pondering this rather hopeless situation which happened in 1929.

he managed to start up the cranky little engine and make it all the way to Port Ludlow before his fuel ran out. There, with the help of local Indians he gathered enough cords of wood to get him to Nanaimo B.C., where he was denied coal but was able to round up additional supplies. Next, he went to the town's abandoned coal dump and again hired some Indians, this time to gather 12 tons of waste coal dust. Steaming yet farther north to seek wood to mix with the coal dust, he encountered a sinking sloop with a crew begging to be rescued. Jones obliged, but not before removing all the supplies and signing on the men as his crew.

Now, all was ready for the open sea, and passing out through the Strait of Juan de Fuca, the *Jenny Jones* rounded Tatoosh Island and pointed her prow southward. For 25 days, under both steam and sail the vessel moved down the West Coast, all the way to the safety of San Blas, Mexico. With his remaining funds Jones paid his crew wages and promised $625 for the gear and food removed from their stricken craft.

When Jones managed to secure a cargo at Mazatlan, the disgruntled crew demanded their money, in fact, one of them known as ''Black Dutch'' Albert, insisted on $1,000, and to back his claim applied to the U.S. consul to have the steam schooner seized until his demand was met. After Jones made additional token payments to his erstwhile crew, the Mexican government released the *Jenny Jones*. Still the harassment continued, and one day, probably due to the efforts of Black Dutch, Jones discovered that the vessel's rudder was missing, so as to delay his departure.

Frustrated and disgusted, he decided to sell the *Jenny Jones* to Mexican interests for $10,000, and on doing so took passage back to San Francisco aboard the steamer

John L. Stephens. At the end of the gangplank, this fugitive from justice was met by the U.S. marshal and immediately taken into custody. A few weeks later, court was held and the full details of the episode disclosed. The judge was somewhat enthralled by the adventurous escapades of this rogue, as was the general public. The final decision was that Jones had not actually stolen the vessel, but that the marshal, while at Steilacoom had been derelict in his duty by leaving his charge. Jones, accordingly was set free, but in turn the officer's bondsmen were sued for $4,600. The matter dragged on in the courts until 1868, when Captain Jones and the erstwhile engineer of the steam schooner, Charles Hughes, got passage back to Puget Sound to face another trial at Steilacoom. Both were exonerated, the case being officially closed and dumped in ''file 13.''

Again we return to early Port Townsend and a writer and journalist named J. Scott Browne, who once described the city as one, ''built on whiskey.'' Initially he was chastised for such uncomplimentary writings, but later turned into the town hero. He wrote about the ''gin mills'' and ''mad houses'' and often centered on one just beyond Point Hudson as a place where seafaring men, Indians and soldiers gathered en masse to drink, gamble, dance, sing and brawl. He told of the ''floosies'' and how the sailors were rolled and drugged.

Here's one for the memory bank. This is the way milk was picked up from the Carnation Dairy at Mount Vernon and delivered along the banks of the Skagit River, beginning in 1908. The **CARNATION NO. 1** and **CARNATION NO. 2**, gas-powered sternwheelers, with 50 horsepower Frisco engines, drew only a few inches and could go anywhere on the river.

Dwelling on other aspects of the "illicit" waterfront, Browne's words were by no means fiction, for as earlier mentioned, when some of the old waterfront buildings were torn down, secreted trapdoors were uncovered which had once opened onto the beach amid worm-eaten piling. Through them victims of knockout drops were lowered to waiting boats which ferried them out to crew-short windjammers in turn for blood money. When no need for the shanghaied existed, the man was rolled and stripped of everything but his long johns and lay there exposed to tide and weather until he either sobered up or shook off the effects of the drops.

Browne began his series of articles in *Harper's* Magazine as early as 1856, and later they appeared in news form under the title, "Crusoe's Island," describing "the city built by whiskey." He pointed the finger at the Hudson's Bay Company whom he claimed had imported the whiskey into the settlement, which in turn brought about the construction of gambling establishments, "whore houses" and other dens of iniquity. His articles

Big innovation — air service to Bremerton from Seattle's central waterfront in the 1920's. The Gorst Air service plane presents a contrast with the Kitsap steamer **VERONA,** coming into her pier.

You've got to be kidding? The **KING COUNTY** of Kent? Photos don't lie. This miserable old sidewheeler, built at Seattle in 1900, was perhaps the first "genuine" ferryboat for Lake Washington service. She ran onto a mudbank at her launching and stranded the county officials aboard, for several hours. Nor was her operation much more successful — less than a decade — before she had her engines removed and the hull left in ignominy. The 115 foot shuttler operated for most of her years between Madison Park and Kirkland on Lake Washington, under the guidance of King County.

One could almost reach out and milk a cow in this country scene as the spirited little steamer **MAY BLOSSOM** made her way up the Sammamish Slough to Bothell from Lake Washington. They say we would never want to go back to the way it was. Hmmmm!

even told of the undesirable odors, uninviting streets and disreputable surroundings. Written with his inimitable touch of satire, people across the country read his words with intense interest. All the while the city fathers grew more furious. The worldly crowd loved it. Browne answered his critics by informing them that the adverse publicity had actually worked in reverse, bringing in more people and more business. And in some ways the writer was correct, for Port Townsend became the jumping off port for the Cariboo gold strike and the destination of scores of tourists who just came in for a "look see."

Browne's rebuttal endeared him to many, and on his return to the "portal of whiskey," a special parade was staged in his honor. He was marched through the streets and offered generous amounts of the same kind of whiskey he claimed had built the town.

The more refined element of Port Townsend, however, was in no way impressed.

Another unsavory character who victimized sailors in the early years had his shingle out at Port Gamble. He was a dentist, and in front of his establishment was a sign;

SAILORS! TAKE NOTICE!

Remember, there are no dentists at sea! Don't start on a long voyage with bad teeth. I will give you a free examination and tell you frankly whether your teeth need attention or not.

This unsavory dentist specialized in extractions, and focused his practice on seafaring men. Whenever a ship was about to sail from the harbor but was short of seamen, the questionable extractor of teeth would receive the word. The immediate patient would then get an overdose of ether and before the effects had worn off would be well out to sea, with or without his toothache.

At the sailors' boarding houses the seaman frequently came out the loser. Though upright skippers usually filled empty berths in a legal way, the tyrant masters were not particular how they got extra hands. Boarding houses were ripe for illegal practices, and despite efforts to keep away from the "hellships," sailors would often end up prostrate on their decks.

One notorious vessel was the bark *Guy C. Goss*. She carried a shipmaster who was a scoundrel and extremely adept at using a belaying pin on any who balked at his orders. The owners of the *Goss* had sadly neglected the once proud Downeaster, allowing her to become unseaworthy and rotten. On one occasion before the turn of the century, the steamer *Al-ki* neared Port Townsend with a group of seamen from Seattle who had been sold a bill

126

Central Seattle waterfront, several decades back, showing the old pioneer Seattle fireboat **SNOQUALMIE,** and the classic waterfront firehouse, right. The white collar steamer **KITSAP** of Kitsap County Transportation Co. is at the Colman dock, and uptown (in the center photo), is pictured the swank Savoy Hotel.

of goods about signing on a "family ship," which afforded the finest or working conditions. In order to receive pay for his passengers, the skipper had to deliver them personally, For fear they might find out about the "hellship" and take a "French leave," he anchored his ship in the harbor. During the night, however, the word leaked out, and three of the men who had knowledge of the *Goss* jumped overboard and struck out for the beach. One of the trio was a good swimmer and was able to cover the distance in spite of the frigid waters, but the other two were on the verge of drowning when their frantic calls brought a rescue vessel. Guess where they ended up? Only the strong swimmer escaped the *Goss* and her tyrant skipper, he doing a quick fadeout on reaching terra firma.

Not only did new hands fear the treatment accorded aboard the *Guy C. Goss,* but one of the regular crew who decided he had had enough, tried another avenue of escape. William Brown was his name, victim of much cruel treatment by both skipper and mates. To get off, as the bark lay in the harbor, he pleaded illness, but his pleas fell on deaf ears. When his request was denied, he grabbed a meat cleaver from the galley and proceeded to cut off one of his fingers. With blood flowing freely from the wound, he was ushered off to the local Marine Hospi-

tal for treatment and the *Goss* was forced to sail without his services.

On another occasion, two seamen jumped overboard from the ship *Benjamin Sewell* of Bath, while she was anchored at Port Townsend's ballast dumping grounds. Just as were those who tried to escape from the *Goss,* they were rescued in drowning condition by a revenue cutter and returned to their ship. Their unsuccessful attempt brought even rougher treatment down on them during the voyage that followed. Further, they learned the hard way that winter time on Puget Sound is no place for swimmers.

The *Goss* and *Sewell* were but two of the many sailing vessels listed on the *Red Record,* a list of notorious ships published in the *Coast Seaman's Journal* of San Francisco. The publication was founded by crusading seafarer Andrew Furuseth, and edited by Walter Macarthur, dedicated to a continuing effort to annex fair treatment for the neglected American seaman. From 1886 to 1895, the *Red Record* (Ecce! Tyrannus) was a summary of some of the cruelties perpetrated upon American seamen, "the symbol of discipline on the American hellship." The sheet more than accomplished its purpose, and slowly brought about the Maguire and White Acts, starting the abused hand before the mast on his way to just and proper treatment.

127

Seattle's waterfront probably about 1919, showing Pier 9, known as Gaffney Dock and Pier 10, the Virginia Street Dock. The big sailing vessel is the well known **ABNER COBURN**, dating from 1882. At her left is the Reliable Oyster and Fish Co. dock. Note wooden stock anchor on the **COBURN**. To orient the reader, these are the veteran piers recently torn down to make room for Seattle's new waterfront aquarium, known as Piers 60-61. They were raised in March of 1975.

Some of the well known hell-ships on the *Red Record,* familiar to Puget Sound waters were the *Susquehanna, Bohemia, Benj. F. Packard, May Flint, Hecla, Francis, Shenandoah, M. P. Grace, Tam O'Shanter, Sterling, Reuce, Standard, Edward O'Brien, Commodore T. H. Allen, Lewellyn J. Morse,* and numerous others.

In Furuseth's paper, the ship, her master, the incident of cruelty and the outcome, before the shipping commissioner, was listed. Charges brought by mistreated seamen, were almost always thrown out of the court hearing, the owners and ships' officers always having the last say. The Coast Seaman's Union was organized to fight against the powerful Shipowners' and Coast Boarding Masters' associations. A titanic battle was begun in the 1890's, one destined to restore to the merchant sailor his proper rights.

A vintage photo taken aboard the new schooner **MABEL GALE,** under construction at the Hall yard at Port Blakely, on Bainbridge Island, 1902. Pictured on the deck of the yet uncompleted 762 ton vessel is Henry K. Hall, the bewhiskered gentleman, a guiding light behind the progressive shipyard which turned out 108 vessels at Port Ludlow and Port Blakely from 1873 till 1903.

Dockton, a weathered settlement at Quartermaster Harbor, Vashon Island, was named by the Puget Sound Dry Dock Company in 1891. The following year, it became the scene of great activity as a drydock, 325 feet long and 182 feet wide was put in operation, becoming known as both the DeLion and later the Heffernan Drydock. The facility repaired many tall sailing vessels and steamers. Boxcars were towed into Quartermaster Harbor by barge and returned to Tacoma with dried codfish, and bricks from the brickyards around the bay. When industrial centers rose elsewhere on Puget Sound, Dockton became a pale ghost, and never recovered again. In the upper photo, the big British four-masted bark **OLIVEBANK** is seen high on the drydock about the year 1906. The vessel later loaded 2.5 million board feet of lumber at Bellingham. In the lower photo, a sizable steamer undergoes repairs at the Heffernan dock. In the foreground are the remains of the abandoned steamer **FLEETWOOD**.

The big British windship **BLYTHSWOOD** is seen in a rare view along the Seattle waterfront, around the turn of the century, drying her sails. Built in 1875, by R. Duncan & Co., the 260 foot vessel, boasting a lovely figurehead of a fair maiden, roamed the seas until 1921 when she was abandoned on fire as the **LYSGLIMT**, under the Danish flag.

James G. McCurdy, in his, *By Juan de Fuca's Strait,* tells of a nefarious character on the Port Townsend waterfront by the name of Sunderstrand, a runner by trade and a scheming renegade, big, powerful and also extemely handy with his fists. Well up on all tricks of the trade, he was a champion at stealing a ship's crew, and for blood money supplying a "needy ship," passing it off as fairplay and legitimate enterprise. Scourge of the Port Townsend waterfront, he was both feared and hated. On one occasion he and his assistant, Harry Stubley, rowed out to a British square-rigger lying off Point Hudson and through bribes and false promises persuaded several members of the crew to desert. Overhearing the tainted words of Sunderstrand, the infuriated skipper, ordered his mate, the bos'n and two others to lower a boat and take out in pursuit of the intruders. Sunderstrand and Stubley were soon overtaken and a general melee erupted as the men in the two craft went to "war." The iron-jawed Sunderstrand stood up like a bull moose, let out a war cry, and swung his oar with such gusto, that had not the mate ducked it would have taken off his head. The officer in turn fired a pistol at his assailant, but missed the mark and instead struck Stubley in the head, leaving a deep wound from which blood gushed. The battle ended abruptly and Sunderstrand rowed his badly wounded companion to shore,

while the English officer assembled his men and returned to their ship.

That night, despite hospital treatment, Stubley died, and immediately law officers went out to the British ship and placed her first officer under arrest, slapping him in the city jail. In the ensuing trial, it was found that Sunderstrand's act was tantamount to "attempted piracy upon the high seas," and the officer was exonerated.

The notorious runner, who gained little sympathy then pleaded his innocence on the grounds that he had not boarded the British ship and that those he had induced to leave had agreed to do so of their own free will. The case attracted much attention, the court room being haunted by an array of waterfront characters, as well as the town's upper echelon determined to see that justice was done. Unfortunately, Sunderstrand's plea got him off. The law, however, rode herd on the burly runner and he was obliged to temper his ways.

Maritime personalities on the more positive side were those, such as the earlier mentioned Chief Seattle, (Sealth) who, with renowned pioneer physician Dr. David S. Maynard struck up a lasting friendship. Talk about an odd couple. The old chief headed the Suquamps (Suquamish) and other local tribes while the doctor took care of the medical needs of the earlier settlers. But, both were versatile, and it was the chief that induced Dr. Maynard to move from Olympia to Seattle in March 1852. He further got him interested in an exporting venture, by teaching him the Indian way of packing salmon in brine. Maynard then reasoned that the preservation of the salmon might make it possible to ship it to San Francisco. So it was that a new trade got started, slow and undependable at first but improved on in later decades.

The old chief who became a staunch friend of the white settlers was born on Blake Island, and as a child witnessed the arrival of Captain Vancouver's ship *Discovery*. When converted to Christianity, he was christened Noah Sealth. At his death at age 80, he was laid to rest at Suquamish by white settlers and his native tribesmen. His epitath read:

Seattle — Chief of the Suquamps and allied tribes. Died June 7, 1866.

History claims that Dr. Maynard, because of his friendship and admiration of the chief, was instrumental in naming the struggling port city in his honor. Because of the difficulty of translating the Indian language, a corruption of the name, came out as Seattle, and Seattle it remained. If the old chief could see the sprawling metropolis that bears his name today, he would probably turn over in his grave in unbelief.

Port Townsend in 1870, as pictured in a print from Harper's Magazine. Located strategically, at the turn from the Strait of Juan de Fuca into Admiralty Inlet and Puget Sound, it was thought that one day Port Townsend would become the principal port and city on the shores of greater Puget Sound. Though playing a lead role in the early maritime history of the area, soon fate ruled that her future would remain nominal, perhaps due to the fact of being so distant from any rail connections. Early Port Townsend catered to scores of tall sailing ships and was also the steamer destination for vessels crossing the Strait from Victoria, B.C. Port Townsend was infamous for its "little Barbary Coast," akin in many respects to that of early San Francisco.

Dr. Maynard, a true example of an enterprising pioneer was not only a fine physician but was an outdoorsman as well. He and men like A. A. Denny with their double-bitted axes felled tall firs and cedars at the early Seattle settlement and rolled the logs by hand either into Elliott Bay or right to the limits of Yesler's Mill. All such laborious work was done by hand until oxen or plow horse teams helped ease the burden. When labor became acute and demands grew, several of the local Indians were converted to lumberjacks and often gave a fine account of themselves.

The initial cargo of piles exported from Puget Sound reputedly went out on the British brig *Rosalind,* and from one of the least known islands on Puget Sound — Anderson Island — at the south end of the inland sea. The recipient was a merchant in Victoria B. C. The island was named by the Wilkes Expedition of 1841 for Alexander Caulfield Anderson, chief trader of the Hudson's Bay Company. Another English ship, the *Albion,* lifted one of the first cargo of spars, well almost, and thereby hangs our next tale.

Eben B. Dorr, U.S. revenue inspector, who in 1850 had briefly seized the Hudson's Bay ship *Caboro* for illegally taking without just compensation, timber from American territory, permanently arrested the *Albion* for a more serious infraction of the same offense. The ship had been sent out from England with orders to bring back a cargo of masts to be used by the British Navy. In command of Captain Richard O. Hinderwell, with William Brotchie as supercargo, the vessel pursued her mission in Pacific Northwest waters. Brotchie had been several years in the employ of the Hudson's Bay Company and as former skipper of the steamer *Beaver,* was totally familiar with every place on Puget Sound and in Canadian waters, including a reef off Victoria which yet bears his name (Brotchie's Ledge) on which the *Albion* once stranded. It was Brotchie who had gone to England to persuade the owners of the *Albion* to come to the Northwest with a contract from the British Admiralty to supply masts and spars. Instructions were for Captain Hinderwell and Brotchie to secure the cargo on Vancouver Island where permission had been granted "to cut timber at ten pounds sterling per load, and to traffic with the Indians for their labor, but not for furs." Brotchie was then to find a safe anchorage on the north side of the Strait and "proceed with a boat, well armed and manned, up to Port Discovery and examine the harbor and wood," to see if suitable timber, could be easily removed, and to use his "own discretion whether you load your spars there or not." Further, he was instructed to find out if he could buy forest land cheap, and with a good title. He was authorized to buy a square mile of land and to leave someone there to retain possession. In other words he was to find a place where good spars were available for a cheap price on the American side.

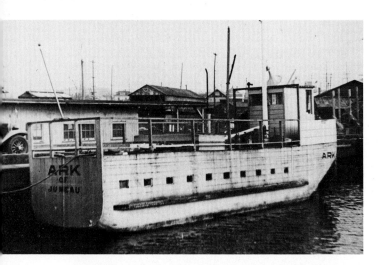

Screwball boats. As long as man has gone down to the sea, he has done it in his own way. Sometimes it borders on the eccentric. There have been many strange craft originated on the waters of Puget Sound over the decades, but among the oddest are the two pictured here. Top, the **ARK** built by a man with a huge family and virtually no money. His goal was to get his clan to Juneau, Alaska and promise of employment. He and his hands put the craft together and had one epic voyage filled with every problem in the book. Below, is a boat with the name **CRITIC**, reputedly built around a monstrous log, but of the owner and what happened to the craft we have been unable to learn.

The *Albion* probably never dropped her anchor off Vancouver Island, for Brotchie believed the best timber to be on the American side of the Strait and it was at Port Discovery Bay the vessel anchored on December 21, 1849 and readied her crew as lumberjacks. Doing all the work by hand, the timbers had to be "clear of sap, and from 70 to 90 feet in length, square at the butt and very little smaller in the middle." The ship's carpenter William Bolton, directed the operation, and a group of curious Clallam Indians were employed to help drag the timbers to the water's edge. The natives were paid in tobacco, clothing, ornaments, fishhooks, needles, knives etc. To each log was fastened a four inch hemp hawser, and then as many Indians as possible would grab hold and yell, "Naw! Skookum Kanowah!"

Alerted of the undertaking, Inspector Dorr and a small regiment of American soldiers from Steilacoom arrived on the scene forcibly seizing the *Albion* for illegally removing American timber. After four months of sweat and toil, only 17 spars had been taken aboard, at the time of the seizure.

Dorr went with the *Albion* to Steilacoom where he posted papers on her mast against the vehement protests of her captain and supercargo who claimed no knowledge of any custom house on Puget Sound where they might have sought entry or clearance. Further, they insisted they had legally purchased the land from the Indians. All protests fell by the wayside, the authorities anxious to show violators that American law on the new frontier had sharp teeth.

On November 2, 1849, District Attorney Holbrook advised the solicitor of the treasury that a decree of forfeiture had been entered at the last term of the district court held in Clarke County against the British ship *Albion*. The ship, her gear, furnishings, merchandise and goods were to be forfeited for violations of revenue laws. Accordingly, the vessel was placed on the auction block at Steilacoom with marshal Meek doing the officiating. Though the 500 ton vessel was valued at some $50,000 the gavel came down on a scant $1,450, going to a party of Olympia capitalists. Most disappointed of the unsuccessful bidders was a character known as Ol' John McLeod, former engineer on the steamer *Beaver*. He had taken a claim at a spot called "Muck," and might have made himself a fat profit if he could have purchased the *Albion*.

The major stockholder of the newly acquired ship was Major H. A. Goldsborough, who arranged for a cargo of piling, potatoes and a quantity of fresh beef for export to San Francisco. In command of Captain Fay, the vessel departed the Sound her holds full, but by the time she reached her destination much of the beef had turned rancid. The remainder of the cargo was sold for a good profit.

An attempt to sell the vessel met with failure for San Francisco Bay was choked with ships from all over the globe, lying in rows, abandoned and rotting away. Gold fever had beckoned passengers and seafarers alike to seek their fortunes. So the *Albion* joined the ghost fleet serving for awhile as a "lodging house" near the Barbary Coast. One day she was loaded with rocks and sand, towed to the head of the bay and allowed to sink as part of a fill-in project.

Even while she was making her last ocean voyage to California in 1851, the seizure incident caused no little amount of diplomatic urgency between the United States and England. Action was slow in coming. The Secretary of the Treasury, Thomas Corwin issued an order to release the ship and her cargo, upon payment of costs, but the edict arrived to late, the *Albion* already having been sold and at rest on San Francisco Bay.

Chapter Seven
Struggle For Survivial

Sweet is the remembrance of troubles
when you are in safety.
> — Euripides

FROM THE BEGINNING of time, the inferior races have been trampled by the superior. Perhaps one of the saddest chapters in all of our history is the disgraceful treatment of the American Indian. Though in many cases the redman attempted to retain his lands, the progressive march of the Caucasion juggernaut relentlessly pushed him back to a few scattered reservations where he lost most of his incentive to pursue his natural existence.

It is true, that many of the pioneers who came west did not intend evil to come upon the Indian, but after infringing on his rights and trespassing on his lands and being attacked in return, they fought back to preserve their lives. As fightings began, hatred grew, and greed and desire prevailed. As for the inferior race, in this case the Indian, more and more of his land was taken without compensation, the voice of the vanquished gradually growing silent.

As the pioneer settlers moved in by sea and land to the shores of Puget Sound, they usually homesteaded wherever they found a good spot, never considering any compensation for the Indian. Occasionally the government would make feeble attempts to purchase native lands or to compensate Indians for services rendered, but for the most part it was a sham. The "real Americans" were often considered to be "ignorant savages" who lacked the ability to form a united government or to bring their scattered tribes into a single military or defense force. For centuries the Indian had lived off the fat of the land, richly endowed with an abundance of animals and fish, edible roots, fruit and berries and an overabundance of tall trees. Though rival tribes sometimes fought among each other, the Puget Sound Indians were generally as peaceful as any in the country, well satisfied with their land of plenty. They traded goods, but for the most part theirs was a closed world, their most feared enemy being the Haida Indians which would come down from the north in their mighty canoes on raiding parties.

From somewhere in the world, ages ago, this unusual race of people drifted to the shores of Puget Sound. So delightful did they find their surroundings, that, like the Polynesians of Hawaii, they ended their wanderings and settled down — content, but illiterate — one generation paralleling the next.

When the white settlers came, there were differences and sometimes open hostility, but the greater number of serious incursions were not with the local tribes, but with those who resided away from Puget Sound. Almost from the beginning the Indian learned of the "white eyes" bad medicine, in the form of firepower, and it was not long before short-sighted pioneer "traveling salesmen" were selling rifles to the savages. The Caucasion also brought venereal diseases, influenza, measles and smallpox, all of which swept through the Indian tribes with disastrous results. Then, almost from the beginning the Indian was introduced to "firewater," strong drink, which he knew not how to control and which in most cases, controlled him.

All set for an Indian canoe race on Puget Sound in the early days. In the background is the old wooden tug **KATAHDIN.**

Contemporary sketch of the USS **DECATUR** beating her way around Cape Froward, Straits of Magellan in 1854. It was this vessel that was credited with saving early Seattle from an Indian attack in 1856.

Some of the more aggressive chiefs in Washington territory were greatly angered at the unauthorized invasion of the whites and took up weapons in protest. For protection, the early commercial trading vessels were all armed as were the government vessels. Ironically, some of the Indians befriended the settlers, betraying their red brothers to warn of planned attacks or to render assistance. Some did it for trinkets or compensation, others from loyalty and goodwill.

Indian troubles had occurred in both the Columbia River and Puget Sound areas in the 1850's, necessitating an increasing number of troops to be dispatched by the government for the protection of the settlers. A deputy marshal named D. Hunt was one of the unfortunate pioneers murdered at the hands of the Indians; seven miners on their way to Fort Langley, on the Fraser River had been massacred; a white woman was captured and carried away into captivity, etc. It was considered unsafe and unwise for any but armed parties to go anywhere on the waters of Admiralty Inlet, among the islands of the San Juan archipelago, or along the shores of Bellingham Bay. The situation worsened in 1859, when the northern Indians coming down with their big war canoes got brave enough to attack both local Indians and or white settlers, bringing fears of Indian war. Warriors from the Queen Charlotte Islands and the northern British Columbia coastal areas resorted 5,000 strong at Victoria in 1859, and incidents on Smith Island near Port Townsend almost touched off a showdown battle. The white settlers got themselves in a lather at Port Townsend preparing to shoot anything that looked like an Indian, but the Haidas evidently weighed the odds and most of them eventually left southern Vancouver Island for their homeland.

In the interim, those warlike Haidas, not deterred by the threats of the white man came and went, in large or small raiding parties, doing petty mischief and never running from a challenge. Haida war canoes carried sometimes from 50 to 75 warriors. Even the white man's "piah ships" (fire ships) brought no fear to the northern Indians and at times they became downright defiant. The fact that the government had vessels cruising off Northwest shores looking for incursions against the settlers had little effect.

A party of invaders landed near Steilacoom and became so troublesome that settler Lafayette Balch appealed to Army Colonel Silas Casey to have them removed. Casey confronted their leaders but met with a stubborn refusal. Captain Swarthout of the government vessel *Massachusetts,* was in turn told to take the situation in hand. By the time the vessel had arrived at Fort Steilacoom the Indians had departed for other areas at the south end of the Sound, one segment becoming involved in a hand-to-hand battle with a local tribe at Henderson Bay, two of their number reportedly being killed.

The *Massachusetts* stalked the Haida war canoes all over Puget Sound but they were crafty navigators and were able to elude the big warship. Finally a large party of the renegades were found encamped near Port Gamble. Swarthout brought his ship to anchor near the encampment and sent Lieutenant Young to have a parley, requesting them to leave the country. The young officer even made an offer to tow the canoes back to Vancouver Island. When this failed he invited three of their chiefs to come aboard and talk with the captain. All of the requests were made from the ship's boat, as the Indians gathered en masse on the beach threatening the lives of any who dared step ashore. Young was obliged to retreat,

Chief (Sealth) Seattle, friend of the white man, for whom the city is named, was chief of the Duwamish tribe, a branch of the Nisqually family of Indians which inhabited the lands rimming many parts of Puget Sound from the Skokomish River at the head of Hood Canal to and beyond the Skagit River. The old gentleman was a man of wisdom and peace, and one who helped start commerce from Puget Sound.

Isaac I. Stevens, first governor of Washington Territory. Born at Andover, Mass., March 28, 1818, he graduated from West Point Military Academy in 1839. After an illustrious career in the Army he was placed in charge of the Coast Survey Office in Washington D.C. in 1849 and appointed governor of Washington Territory on March 17, 1853. He later was elected as a delegate to Congress. As a major general with the volunteers, he was killed in the Civil War at Chantilly, Va., September 1, 1863. One of the few bad pieces of advice he afforded during his career, was in telling the early settlers of Seattle there was no danger of an Indian attack. The attack came a few days later.

and retreat he did. Next, the angered Swarthout sent a party consisting of 45 of his best men, plus a howitzer. The offer was repeated. The Haidas remained defiant, stoutly refusing to leave. Again the party returned to their ship. That night the *Massachusetts,* upped anchor and moved into shallow water just as near the encampment as possible. She was joined by the smaller steamer *Traveler.* Both the latter vessel and a launch from the *Massachusetts* had cannon aboard. All three vessels took

up firing positions determined to catch the Haidas by complete surprise. Endeavoring to prevent bloodshed, Swarthout dispatched Lieutenant Semmes ashore the following morning to reason once more with the "savages." Following a lengthy parley, there was no change in the attitude of the northerners, so the lieutenant landed with 20 soldiers and marines taking with them the howitzer from the launch. But, the Indians already aroused to battle pitch, daringly seized the arms and quickly re-

Would you believe it? This is how the city of Seattle appeared in its youth as a struggling lumber mill settlement in 1864, taken from a photo once in the possession of Clarence B. Bagley. The mill is at the right.

First post office in Tacoma, located at Job Carr's house at Old Town was also the first house built on the townsite, about 1864.

treated to the safety of the forests, taking positions for all-out battle. The gun from the *Traveler* responded with a volley and the enemy returned the fire. The battle was on. The *Massachusetts* then opened up with shell and grapeshot, peppering the forest. This was followed by another broadside, giving Semmes and his regrouped fighters a chance to charge the abandoned camp. They wasted little time destroying it, and then withdrew. Meanwhile the big war canoes lying empty on the beach were fired upon, all but one being blasted to splinters, and that was destroyed later to block any escape. The battle raged on through the day, the Indians taking pot shots at anything that moved within range of their guns. Late that afternoon a captured squaw was sent back to her people with a message from Swarthout that if they would surrender and agree never to return again they would be taken across the Strait. Still undaunted, they sent the old woman back with a blatant "no," that "they would fight as long as there was a man of them alive."

For two more days they held out, but the one thing they had not counted on was the problem of hunger. At last they were compelled to yield. When the battle began, they had 117 warriors plus several women and children. Of that number 27 died, 21 were wounded, one of them a chief. They had lost all their property, even their

war canoes. The "piah ships" had won out again. Like cattle, the sadly defeated, still defiant warriors were herded aboard the *Massachusetts* and taken back to Vancouver Island. There they were landed and furnished meager food and supplies, along with a warning never to return again.

The battle claimed the life of one American and the wounding of another, both of whom were attached to the warship.

The Haidas left promising not to return, but the disastrous defeat left revenge burning in their hearts. They secretly vowed to have a "Boston tyee," (high ranking white) for every warrior killed in battle.

The following summer, a party of 200 northern Indians camped on Whidbey Island. Some of their number made an unauthorized visit to the home of Colonel Isaac Ebey, and were received in friendship. During the night, they returned, calling the colonel to the door. There, he was gunned down in cold blood, his head brutally cut off and carted away as a trophy. In the house at the time were Mrs. Ebey, her three children, and George W. Corliss and his wife. Frantically, amid a hail of bullets, they escaped, hiding in the dark shadows of the tall trees. The Indians gave no chase and did no further dastardly acts against any other island settlers. Instead, in typical In-

Whidbey Island blockhouse (still standing) was built during the Indian War near the claim which Colonel I. N. Ebey had taken, and where he was subsequently murdered by the northern Indians (Haidas). They visited his house prior to the murder and were received kindly. Next day the savages did their dastardly act, shot him, cut off his head and carried it away in revenge for a skurmish earlier at Port Gamble when American soldiers from the USS **MASSACHU-SETTS** and the steamer **TRAVELLER** (in 1854), fought a pitched battle with the Indians who had come in large war canoes, 117 strong, plus women and children. The battle was fought mostly on land and the Haidas lost 27 warriors and another 21 were wounded. Most of their canoes were shot up while lying on the beach.

dian fashion, they vanished from the island taking their bloodied trophy with them — the first of the vowed ''Boston tyees,'' in revenge for their warriors that perished in the Port Gamble battle. They still had 26 more to gain and were only willing to settle for high ranking military officers and prominent settlers. It was also believed that they were seeking revenge for the killing of a northern Indian at the hands of settlers on Budd Inlet, three years earlier.

Late in January 1859, another regrettable tragedy credited to the northern Indians, undoubtedly out of revenge, involved two small Yankee trading vessels — the schooner *Blue Wing* owned by Ernest Schroter, and the *Ellen Maria,* skippered by Captain McHenrie. Both departed Steilacoom for Port Townsend on January 25, 1859, but neither ever reached its destination. Despite a search no trace of the two craft could be found. Then in April, an Indian reported to authorities at Steilacoom that a boat had been burned at the north end of Vashon Island, and her crew murdered. The report was followed up, and piece by piece the heinous crime was put together. A Haida war canoe composed of ten warriors and

five squaws had attacked the *Blue Wing* off Vashon Island, and after killing her crew, stripped the craft of its wares and scuttled it to hide the traces.

Next, the hostiles turned their vengeance toward the *Ellen Maria*, her crew being oblivious to the earlier atrocity. Captain McHenrie was more cautious, and knowing the warlike ways of the Haidas, ordered the canoe away by waving his rifle in the air as they came near in an attempt to board. When the Indians refused to back off, the schooner's master opened up, killing the brother of much feared ''Hydah Jim,'' a well known chief. He also wounded another of their number. Quickly, the canoe pulled away from the *Ellen Maria,* but the iron was in the fire. By nightfall, the war canoe returned, as if on cat's paws. Undetected, the warriors boarded at will, and bludgeoned the small crew to death. Next, they stripped the craft of its wares, ran her up on the beach and celebrated their double victory by burning the vessel to the water's edge.

Before dawn, the attackers had left the scene of their triumph, their canoe loaded down with many prizes. It was as if they vanished into the still, haunting fog hang-

Port Townsend and its harbor at the turn of the century. Over top of Indian and Marrowstone islands can be seen Whidbey Island and sections of Admiralty Inlet. Redding's photo.

ing over Sound waters. The story might never have been revealed except for the local Indian who allegedly watched the ship burning from a distant hill.

Where troubles with the northern Indians continued from time to time there was also occasional hostility shown by the tribes in Washington Territory. Ocean steamships and river boats were employed to transport troops to wherever an Indian uprising was reported. Steilacoom, near old Fort Nisqually, was the headquarters for troop movements on Puget Sound, and the steamers *California* and *Republic* made several trips north from San Francisco in the 1850's on behalf of the government who had long feared an Indian uprising. Governor Douglas at Victoria, B.C. also placed at the disposal of the Americans, the venerable steamer *Beaver,* in case of an emergency.

Warlike Klikitats were rumored sighted more than 100 strong on the prairie, near Fort Nisqually. News then arrived at Olympia that Chief Leschi, with a force of 38 hostiles was visiting an Indian reservation on Fox Island where Indian agent John Swan was reportedly being held as a hostage. Leschi was recruiting all able-bodied Indians to go on the warpath, and was also rumored to have carried his recruiting activities to the Squaxin Island Indian encampment. The initial report proved false, but the latter two proved true, for indeed Leschi was drumming up activity for battle against the whites.

As excitement increased, the most frightened parties were the isolated pioneer families, who were often open targets for sneak attacks. The survey steamer *Active* arrived from San Francisco, with arms and ammunition

and other government vessels patrolled Sound shores with orders to keep on the alert for any acts of hostility. Among them was the sloop-of-war *Decatur,* the revenue cutter *Jefferson Davis* and the steamers *John Hancock* and *Massachusetts* in addition to the *Active.* Local Indians meanwhile carefully observed the movement of troops and ships by means of their primitive but effective grapevine wireless.

When new Indian activity was reported on the South Sound islands, most of the Yankee ships were elsewhere, so the *Beaver* was dispatched to Fort Nisqually and given orders to "approach the island and put 30 armed men ashore with instructions to capture Leschi, if possible, and to destroy all his boats."

Unable to land, due to shoal water, the soldiers were unable to establish a beachhead, and with no cannon aboard the *Beaver,* the expedition was a total failure. Leschi and his braves laughed loudly at the inability of the military force to function.

Captain E. D. Keyes, USA, who was in command of the landing party, was unable to foresee the cunning chief's plans were by no means confined to the lower Puget Sound area. The vindictive Indian, was fighting for a cause, and that cause was to get the entire Puget Sound country back to its rightful owners. He had allied his activities with the other tribes that shared a similar view, though many labeled him as only an "agitator." Whatever his faults and shortcomings, he believed in a free hand for his people.

Within three weeks of the south Sound incident, Klikitats were crossing Snoqualmie Pass, following a

Arthur A. Denny, who crossed the plains to Oregon Territory, from Illinois arrived at Portland in 1851. Born in Indiana in 1822, this pioneer later boarded the schooner **EXACT,** while at Portland, and sailed to Puget Sound where with a small band of other settlers he landed at Alki Point, near what would later become Seattle, on November 13, 1851. As a representative of the territory, a lieutenant during the Indian wars, and progressive empire builder, he was on the committee that officially named Seattle. Further he served as receiver of the land office at Olympia and represented the territory in Congress for one year.

The Reverend Daniel Bagley, born in Pennsylvania in 1818, crossed the plains to Oregon, and in 1860 moved to Seattle, where he played an active role in the founding and upbuilding of the territorial university and in other progressive ventures in Seattle.

A pioneer who played an enlightening role in waterfront and railroad progress in early Seattle was James M. Colman, a Scotsman, born in 1832, and who came to Puget Sound in 1861. As a master machinist he not only built several lumber mills on the Sound but invented some advanced machinery to up their production. He led the drive to build the railroad out of Seattle up to the rich coal mining sections in 1875.

The thriving capital city of Olympia has changed abruptly over the years. It's hard to believe that scenes such as this were common at the settlement two decades before the turn of the century. American settlers first arrived at nearby Tumwater in 1845 and at Olympia, two years later.

secret parley with Leschi. They planned to attack Seattle in conjunction with a similar strike at Steilacoom.

An earlier incursion near the Stuck and White rivers had involved some 300 warlike Indians, mostly Nisqually led by Quiemuth and Kitsap, and the Klikitats under Chief Kanasket. One Indian had been killed after 32 horses and mules belonging to the settlers had been run off and taken by the attackers. A tragic aftermath was the shooting of Army lieutenant W. A. Slaughter who was picked off by the Indians as he entered his cabin door.

Increased troop activities near Steilacoom evidently changed Leschi's attack plans, but elsewhere the Klikitats had successfully assembled the largest party of hostile Indians that ever were to attack any site on Puget Sound. They had crossed the pass, bent on the destruction of fledgling Seattle, which in 1856 consisted of a sawmill, a few cabins, some stores, and nearby farms. The area had been cleared of trees, though the stumps remained. Most of the structures stood just above the tideflats, one end of which had been filled with sawdust from the mill. At one corner of the town was a crudely constructed blockhouse for protection against surprise attack. In the wake of the earlier White River massacre there was of course, concern. Some 14 settlers — men, women and children — had been murdered at the hands of the Indians in the White River Valley, near where Kent and Auburn are presently located. The attacking party was reputedly led by a White River Indian known as Nelson, a man who was thought to be a friend of the settlers, having received many favors from them in the early 1850's.

Several of Seattle's male citizens had gone to join Captain Hewitt in defense of the hard-hit White River settlers, and were just now returning. Eastward of the settlement, the forest remained uncut, except for a small opening where a narrow trail led to Lake Duwamish, the original name for Lake Washington. Totally undetected the Indians, with great cunning, had entrenched themselves among the trees preparing for their attack. The fly in-the-ointment to their plans was the sloop-of-war *Decatur* anchored in Elliott Bay. From the time of her October arrival the warship had been cruisng northward and southward along the shores of Puget Sound, her mission, to keep all Indians from attacking white settlers.

Ironically, a few weeks before coming to Seattle, the *Decatur* had stranded on an uncharted rock at slack tide off Bainbridge Island. Receiving considerable damage to her bottom timbers, she limped across the Sound to Seattle with her pumps going constantly. There she was beached near Yesler's Mill where her ship's carpenters mended the damage. In the interim, Captain Guver Gansevoort replaced Captain J. S. Sterret as the ship's commander. The former, fortunately was a very cautious individual.

The townsmen were by no means unanimous concerning the danger of an Indian attack, despite the fact that during the previous September, Chief Sealth had warned the settlers that hostile Indians were planning to come from east of the mountains to wipe out Seattle. His words had been taken lightly except by the more cautious God-fearing citizens who called a special prayer meeting to ask God's protection. Many felt that the *Decatur's* arrival was indeed the Lord's answer to their plea, and as it turned out, it proved to be so.

North of the blockhouse resorted a small encampment of friendly Indians who had come and gone at will ever since the settlers arrived. Their chief, known as "Curley," boasted of his friendship with the pioneers and had always insisted that he would warn them of hostile actions by other tribes. Like many of the Puget Sound Indians, Curley, burned the candle at both ends. Whatever course appeared to be most promising was the course he would take. If the existing situation favored the white man, he was on the white man's side, but if the situation favored the Indian, he took that side. Though he was constantly playing the role of informer, many of the settlers did not trust him, in fact, Gansevoort and his officers had gained an immediate mistrust of the fickle chief. Instead, they put their reliance on another informant known as "Indian Jim," a close friend of settler D. Williamson. He had reiterated Chief Sealth's earlier warning and further told of planned attacks on both Seattle and Steilacoom. He further revealed that Owhi, one of Kam-i-ahkan's principal warriors would lead the Klikitat war party. When asked by the ship's commander how many Indians would be involved, he answered,

Two wide-angle views of the Port Blakely Mill Co. and Port Blakely harbor as of March 26, 1918. As can be seen, the little island port was still going strong right up through World War I, the big commercial sail carriers getting in their last cargoes before the steamers crowded them off the seas.

'hiu,'' which translated from the Chinook tongue means ''very many.''

Inasmuch as no hostile activities had been observed little alarm was registered by the settlers. A token guard was kept along the banks of the Duwamish River and at the head of the bay, but nobody was apprised of a possible attack from the forests. Still, Gansevoort's wisdom prompted him to place a small howitzer on the shore opposite the sandspit, and by nightfall the marine guard

from his ship patrolled a mile along the waterfront and up to the blockhouse. Some of the settler's laughed at such extreme precautions, and none more than Governor Isaac I. Stevens, Washington Territory's first governor, who had just returned from Blackfoot Country. At the time, he was making a tour of Puget Sound aboard the *Active,* and on January 24, 1856, the ship called at Seattle, during which time he took the occasion to address the settlers. During his speech he made the foolish statement

"Hey brudda, which way I go?" Looking somewhat like a Chinese puzzle, the Seattle waterfront tideflat was a maze of rail trestles and deadend roads in the early days. Much of the area here has since been filled in. The factory at the center of the photo, is the Seattle Box Company. The West Seattle area is in the background.

that, "New York and San Francisco were not safer from attack than Seattle was at the moment."

Even as he spoke, the Indians were entrenched by the hundreds just above the town awaiting the opportune time to strike.

Indian Jim, in the interim revealed that some of the hostiles had favored attacking while the sloop-of-war was repairing on the beach, reasoning that it could have been easily boarded and plundered. This, he said, had brought controversy among them, the opposition favoring waiting until the vessel was at anchor in the bay and most of her crew asleep. The informant claimed he had been at the parley when the Indians voted to take the latter course of action.

Came the chill, clear night of January 25, 1856. It was quiet at the settlement. The soldiers and marines were on the alert. The pastoral scene was disturbed at 10 p.m. by an owl's hoot coming from the direction of the forest. This was followed by another from a different location. Those wise in Indian ways reasoned them to be signals. Morning came and the guard was disbanded, returning to the ship for breakfast. No sooner had they lifted their coffee mugs than orders came to get back to the beach, immediately. Captain Gansevoort, who had

not once relaxed his vigil, was scanning the shore with his glass and had noted unusual activity at the so-called friendly Indian camp above the settlement. Greatly disturbed, he joined his guardsmen ordering them to take up their positions and to hold them at any cost. Then he gave word to fire a howitzer round in the direction of a settler's farm at the upper outskirts of the village, while at the same time the ship's cannon lobbed a ball into the woods. By doing so, the canny commander made the enemy play its hand. Immediately, a volley of gunfire was returned from several "timbered arsenals," accompanied by wild calls and beating drums. The Indians were again on the warpath.

As instructed, the women and children ran for the blockhouse while members of the Hewitt army contingent sought their rifles. The *Decatur* now lay broadside to the town, cannon with teeth bared. As the Indians reloaded their rifles after the first round, the settlers took advantage of a few precious moments and ran for safety. The entire population was small, in fact there were only 175 whites who could take up arms, including 120 attached to the *Decatur*. All that kept the Indians from swooping down from their forest stronghold was the fear of the warship's guns, which had proven to be far more

142

powerful than any they had ever known. Throughout most of the day the firing continued from both sides. The town was sprayed with a variety of ammunition but damage was minimal. The settlers were now well concealed and the Indian rifle fire was falling in some cases, much short of the mark.

Solid shot and charges of grape and shrapnel were fired from the *Decatur* and from the shore guns. All day big hunks of land were torn up and tall trees splintered. Though the defenders were outnumbered about ten to one, their confident and spunky pioneer women urged them on to victory.

Along about noon there came a lull in the fighting, the Indians easing up for a feast of steaks prepared by their women folk. The meat was ''courtesy'' of the settlers, having been purloined by the Indian braves early in the battle. While the warriors licked their chops, the let up in the fighting prompted the removal of the white women and children from the blockhouse to the *Decatur,* and to the ship *Brontes* lying in the bay awaiting a cargo of lumber. This was done as a safety precaution. Some personal belongings were also removed from the settlers' homes and buildings for fear the Indains would touch the torch to the settlement by nightfall which was just what they had in mind. On seeing the latter action, the Indians opened fire with everything they had scattering the settlers in every direction.

At one point in the fighting, the attackers gathered near the trail head for a rush against the outer guard of 14 marines. When hesitating, the badly outnumbered men defending the perimeter of the circle, countercharged, driving the Indians back to the protection of the forest. Had the braves not retreated, they might have well broken through the defense line and swept down on the town. It was a standoff throughout the afternoon, neither side showing any progress. The ship's ''fireballs'' were of a magnitude never known to the Indians. They fell into woods with a loud roar doing much damage, wounding and killing. The chiefs were greatly distrubed because their ''necromancers'' had nothing to offset the white man's ''bad medicine.''

As the shadows of evening grew longer, the Indians laid their plans to burn the town, but Gansevoort, reasoning their move had his gunners intensify their barrage, firing relentlesssly into the forest, dispersing their incendiaries. By 11 p.m. the attackers apparently had lost their will to continue to fight. At dawn all was quiet on the western front; the woods were empty. Only a few houses nearest ''no man's land'' had been burned, the Indians mysteriously disappearing, their only trophies, a considerable amount of stolen livestock.

Only two defenders of Seattle had been killed, Robert Wilson, who was shot while fighting from behind a stump, and Milton Holgate, near the backdoor of the blockhouse. The Indian casualty report was never revealed, although reports claimed 28 died and 80 were wounded. In native tradition, the dead had been carried away from the battle scene. Lieutenant Phelps from the

Construction of Harbor Island into an industrial area for the port of Seattle and other industries. Note wooden plank road. The view is to the north before the erection of the present facilities of the Todd Shipbuilding yard.

Contrasts on the early Seattle waterfront. The upper photo was probably taken in the late 1870's showing several sailing vessels in to load lumber at Yesler's mill, and another in the background waiting to load coal. At the very center of the photo, is the remains of the bark **WINDWARD,** wrecked at Useless Bay on Whidbey Island in 1875 and eventually towed to Seattle and stripped. When the Seattle waterfront was filled in, the hull was covered over and today lies approximately under the old Colman Annex on Western Avenue. In the other photo, taken by photographer Wilse in 1899, there appears to be a traffic jam on the Seattle waterfront. Foreground left, is the square-rigged Downeaster **C.F. SARGENT,** out of Bath, Maine. The other vessels are the steamships, **UMATILLA, ALKI** and the **WALLA WALLA,** all prominent coastwise or Alaska passenger vessels.

Early scene of the Seattle waterfront, showing old Denny Hill and Washington Hotel in the background. The hill in later years was completely leveled to form the Denny Regrade. Behind Denny Hill is Queen Anne Hill. Note the scores of passenger and utility craft on the waterfront which for many years were the main transportation to all Sound ports from Seattle. The two large piers in the background, No. 3 and 5 were owned by Northern Pacific Railroad.

Decatur, who had been in charge of the shore contingent estimated that perhaps 1,000 Indians had taken part in the fracas; others guessed the figures to be lower.

The ability of the Klikitats to sneak in quietly and vanish as if into thin air, was almost mystical. Some made their way back over the pass while others took up with Leschi and his braves going again up the White River Valley to plunder and burn settlers' houses. Within two days, the smarting Indians saw to it that no house was left standing in King County, except at the Seattle and Alki areas. But for the *Decatur,* the hostiles would have taken not only Seattle but all of King County and beyond, and had the attack been made while the ship was on the beach, they would have probably plundered her as well in a bloody do-or-die fracas. Perhaps the greatest stumbling block to the nefarious scheme, aside from the sloop-of-war, was the dependable informant, Indian Jim.

Captain Gansevoort, who deserved a medal for his wise vigilance, was delivered a message by an Indian runner a few days later. It warned that he, Chief Leschi would return in a month and conquer the town. As of that moment there was no hesitation on behalf of the settlers in taking every possible precaution against future incursions. Mill owner, Henry Yesler donated an entire ship's load of lumber for a new fortification, and a wooden barricade five feet high was placed all around the border of the town. A second blockhouse was also built, the two being connected by a tunnel and a strong stockade. Each blockhouse was provided with two small cannon, one of which was donated by the USRC *Active.*

All the while the governor's face grew redder and redder. His unfortunate advice could have spelled the doom of Seattle. A company of volunteers, some 51 in all, committed to the defense of the settlement, chose Chief Justice Edward Lander as their captain. This time the townsfolk would be ready. Never again was the town attacked, nor did Leschi make good his warning. Several months later, a reward of 50 blankets was offered for information leading to his arrest. Betrayed by one of his own relatives, he was apprehended and tried at Steilacoom, for the cold blooded murder of several white settlers. Though found guilty, his fate hung in the balance, his defense alleging that the murders were done when the Indians, in essence, were in a state of war with the whites. Though postponed several times, the historic case finally ended with the hanging of the chief from a gallows near Fort Steilacoom.

The port settlement of Tacoma was preceded by a little mill village known as Commencement City, where in the middle of the last century, raw logs were rolled in and cut into lumber. For a time the millsite flourished until superseded by Tacoma. Like Seattle, the "city of destiny," also had its problems, and we concern ourselves here with the facts leading up to the coming of the first railroad to Puget Sound country and how Tacoma became its terminus. Railroad developers visioned this south Sound port as the prime city of the entire territory.

When a census of Washington Territory was taken in 1870, Walla Walla County in Eastern Washington was the most populated, boasting a "whopping 5,300 citi-

Descending the foc's'le ladder aboard Admiral Peary's flagship **ROOSE-VELT**, one of Puget Sound country's best known and loved pioneers, Ezra Meeker. Having had much to do with the upbuilding of a frontier land, Meeker lived to a ripe old age. He came west in 1852.

In the early 1920's — the Oriental dock, Everett Terminal No. 1. Two freighters take on lumber, while a sailing vessel loads on the other side of the pier.

zens. King County, locale of Seattle, had only 2,246 people, fourth after Clarke and Thurston counties. From the railroad point of view, Seattle was on the eastside of Puget Sound and therefore considered by many at a disadvantage for a rail terminus, divided from the eastern half of the territory by a mountain chain. It was in addition, further north from the Columbia River than the towns of Olympia, Tacoma and Steilacoom. Port Townsend was considered too far north on the western side of Puget Sound, despite its strategic location for water transportation. The only hope for Seattle appeared to be the conquering of Snoqualmie Pass, the route which the Klikitats followed en route to their attack on Seattle. Such a route had been envisioned as early as 1870, and Governor Stevens, whose face wasn't so red anymore, showed more wisdom by favoring such a project as a means to tie together the eastern and western halves of the territory.

Meanwhile, surveyors were sent out from eastern United States to make surveys for a rail link from Kalama (on the Columbia River) to Puget Sound in addition to eying the mountain pass route. The Jay Cooke & Company had undertaken bond sales on behalf of Northern Pacific Railroad with an other eye toward eventual transcontinental service.

Very slowly the iron rails moved toward the west. A bond drive was started in the summer of 1872 when five members of the rail line's board of directors arrived on Puget Sound intent on selection of a possible terminus. These gents, accompanied by the firm's chief engineer, cruised Puget Sound for a week aboard the steamer *North Pacific* seeking the most promising seaport location. The citizens of Seattle wanted the terminus in the worst way,

offering the firm 7,500 town lots, 1,000 acres of land, $50,000 in cash, $200,000 in bonds, the use of the tidelands and a place for a depot. Nobody else was willing to match such an offer, but the board members were not swayed. They did, however, narrow their choice down to Tacoma, Mukilteo or Seattle. Olympia was ruled out because the receding tide left the port "a wide expanse of mud and mussel shells for half of every 24 hours." Steilacoom appeared to be "on a strait rather than on a good roadstead," and it was emphasized that the terminus must have a good seaport potential so that there could be a direct hookup between water commerce and rail transport. Seattle, they recognized as "a petty lumbering place," objectionable because of its steep hills and lack of level ground for depot yards and sidings.

The visitors desired a location where they could find not only a good harbor, but adequate shore facilities for wharves and inexpensive land for a future city. In the final analysis, Commencement Bay got the temporary nod as most adequately fulfilling the conditions. For the first time, pint-sized Tacoma received the publicity that put it on the map.

By the time the committee returned to New York they found that bond sales had dropped appreciably, and accordingly, financial difficulties followed. The optimistic plan of linking the east and west fell into limbo. R. D. Rice was then named vice president and John C. Ainsworth, of Portland, became managing director for the western division. No official announcement had as yet been made on a Puget Sound terminus though a land company was formed to buy all the available property on the west shore of Commencement Bay in accordance with its grant. After another visit to Puget Sound, the rail officials returned to Kalama and wired the directors in New York that Tacoma had been officially selected as the Sound terminus. Great excitement erupted, for many of the local settlers had feared the announcment might never come. On September 10, 1872 the land company became official, "to form, own, improve and manage the sale of the townsite."

General Morton McCarver, who had come to Oregon with the Burnett-Applegate party in 1843, a speaker of the house of representatives under the provisional government, and commissary general in the Indian wars, was to play a lead role in the venture. He was a relative by marriage to Captain Ainsworth, who in addition to his railroad "ties" was on the management team of the Oregon Steam Navigation Company.

Tacoma's stroke of good fortune had somewhat tainted the thinking of its citizens and promoters. A campaign was started to change the name of Mount Rainier to either Mount Tacoma or Takoma. Disregarding Captain Vancouver's choice for the majestic peak, Tacomans countered with the fact that Siwash Indians had referred to it as "Takoma" centuries before the great explorer arrived. This caused no little amount of friction in com-

peting seaport towns around Puget Sound. Rivalry grew keener.

Even as the right-of-way was extended north from Kalama, the Jay Cooke bonding firm collapsed, and the Northern Pacific found itself once again in financial difficulties. It was nip-and-tuck all the way, but loans finally permitted the laying of the rails all the way to Commencement Bay. It was an historic day when General McCarver drove the last spike at 3 p.m. on the afternoon of December 16, 1873. For the first time, Puget Sound was connected with the Columbia River by a railroad, and though a transcontinental hookup was yet a long way off, progress was being made, and Puget Sound was no longer "land-locked."

Then came trouble with a capital T. After the initial train arrived, the unpaid graders and track layers demanded restitution immediately. The construction company, however, was so deep in debt that no money was forthcoming and the contractors conveniently disappeared. Infuriated, the laborers took over the track, built a barricade and would have dynamited the bridges and ripped up the iron had not Captain Ainsworth intervened. He promised to pay all back wages through his personal

A huffin' and a puffin' over the pass an old Great Northern steam train finds the going rough as it pulls a heavy load of freight cars. The historic rail routes over the Cascade passes were vitally important to the early upbuilding of Puget Sound ports.

Seattle's Railroad Avenue (Alaskan Way) in 1896, when passenger trains were a major form of transportation. In this Wilse photograph the names on the downtown buildings are easily readable.

credit, and after a long parley, tempers temporarily subsided. True to his word, Ainsworth went into hock down to the heels of his socks.

Though having lost out in the bid for a rail terminus, officials of Olympia and Seattle became even more aggressive. In no way did they intend to let Tacoma become the hub of transportation activity on Puget Sound. The traditional "Seattle Spirit" came to the fore with a meeting on the sawdust grounds bordering the old Yesler Mill. All of the town's 1,142 citizens heard attorney Selucius Garfielde, an ex politician, expound that the charter of the Northern Pacific Company, as originally granted, had provided for a main line from a point on the Columbia River near Wallula across the mountains to the Sound, with a branch down the Columbia. He warned of a change by which the Columbia River branch was to become the principal line, making the "real" terminus, the river, and that little if any business would go to any Sound ports but Tacoma. He further insisted the branch from Wallula to Puget Sound would never be constructed. Garfielde then suggested that if Seattle was to survive, it would have to build a track of its own through Snoqualmie Pass, and on the route suggested by Governor Stevens, linking with prosperous Walla Walla county, whereby its products could come directly to Seattle. Though the task appeared almost insurmountable, the attorney raised considerable excitement among his listerners.

Garfielde afforded facts showing the cost of transportation down the river, with its many portages, thence by rail from Kalama to Tacoma would be more costly to shippers than would a narrow guage railroad across the pass between Seattle and Walla Walla.

Almost immediately steps were taken to procure capital for such a venture, the appointed officials being A. A. Denny and John J. McGilvra who were sent to Walla Walla to drum up interest. A company was organized and stock issued. The news media of King, Yakima and Walla Walla counties got behind the crusade and each area where the proposed line was to pass through got on the bandwagon by issuing more bonds to bolster the undertaking. Lands and right-of-ways were made available. As in all such ventures, however, after the initial excitement wore off, interest began to wane. Especially was this true in Walla Walla, where Dr. Dorsey S. Baker already had his "Rawhide Line" under construction, from Walla Walla to Wallula. Some 15 miles of track had been laid, and Baker, naturally made no bones about his opposition to the proposed mountain route, as opposed to the river route. The charter for the Walla Walla Railroad had been granted as early as 1862. So again, the bulk of the burden fell back on the Seattleites, and financing became increasingly more difficult during those panic years. Even Northern Pacific with its huge land grant and approval from Congress was virtually bankrupt and unable to get additional credit.

San Francisco's cable cars had nothing on those that once rode the Yesler cable way. From downtown Seattle to the shores of Lake Washington it was a "hilly" affair but a colorful experience for the riders. These photos were taken shortly before the demise of the Yesler line.

LEONIE

West Side Outing Club - Trip July 17th. 1910

Now, this is the way to do things up in style, at least it was in 1910, in the good ol' summer time when this group went for a Sunday cruise aboard the launch **LEONIE.** They were known as the West Side Outing Club, and they even had their own burgee.

With 300 miles of track to lay, and with the land yet to be surveyed, the mountain pass railroad appeared more and more like a wild pipe dream. James Tilton and T. B. Morris then undertook a survey of the route and by the early part of 1874 handed in their report. It revealed an estimated cost of $14,000 per mile, with a total outlay of $4.2 million if by the lower Yakima route, or $3.7 million via the Priest Rapids route. They further calculated that annual revenue of $1.6 million could be expected just from the hauling of grain and livestock west and coal and lumber eastbound. even with this encouraging report it was hard to attract outside capital, and again it was Seattle's citizens that had to go it alone. But make no mistake, their enthusiasm had not been dampened, for as the Bible says, ''Where there is no vision, the people perish,'' and perish they would not.

On May 1, the entire town turned out to launch the building of their ''own'' railroad. Whistles blew, bells rang and there was merriment in the streets. The lumber mill was shut down and every man, woman and child boarded steamboats, barges and other conveyances to go up river to where the work was to get started, three miles from the proposed Seattle terminus. There, with axes swinging and saws buzzing, land clearing got underway. Everbody worked, even the sluggards dared not lay

down on the job. Merchants, bankers, school teachers and even preachers labored side by side as the women prepared the food and kept an eye on the kids. A goal of 15 miles of road was planned before the winter rains. Though the work continued with a will, rough terrain permitted only 12 graded miles by October. In the interim, the fortitude of the local citizens gained the respect and interest of many outsiders. A San Francisco firm agreed to establish a shipyard and an iron works in Seattle for a subsidy in land; coal mines opened in the foothills near the proposed route, while another group undertook to negotiate a loan of $200,000 to assist in financing the railroad.

Even with all of the encouragement and investment, the project was still in need of more financing. The coffers were running low and the only remaining alternative was to make an appeal for government assistance through the Congress of the United States. Representatives carried the case right to Washington D.C., but all efforts came to naught, especially with Portland citizens on a similar crusade to gain a trans-continental link up with the Union Pacific. Even Northern Pacific was seeking government help, and in addition, was opposed to the Seattle-Walla Walla project. The picture at best was bleak.

In every determined effort, one of great vision arrives on the scene, in this case, James M. Colman, a Scotsman who had come to Puget Sound in 1861. This quiet industrious individual had established several successful lumber mills on the Sound and after superintending the building of the Hanson & Ackerson mill at Tacoma, he came to Seattle, where with others, he leased the Yesler Mill, eventually buying out his partners. By constructing trestles over Seattle's mudflats he created port access between the town and the coal mining district. Urging others to invest, Colman, by March 1877 had the "iron horses" running over the initial segment of the rail line, delivering coal for local consumption and to the waterfront bunkers. One 21 ton locomotive and ten, eight ton coal cars were in service, plus ten flat cars and one combination passenger, baggage and mail car. Ten additional cars were also under construction and an additional small locomotive was running on the upper part of the rail line.

Confidence grew in Colman who had created a prosperous new industry for the town. Many felt with his great initiative he might one day be able to take the line clear over the pass, unless some national rail syndicate beat him to the task.

The good folk of Olympia were also pouring on the steam. In October 1873, Thurston County voted bonds to complete a branch of the railroad from their harbor to the town of Tenino. It was another of those go it alone projects, and as did the Seattleites, Olympians turned out en masse on April 7, 1873, first marching to Tumwater and then clearing land for their "own" railroad. Trees were felled, stumps uprooted as virgin forests were parted. With great determination, the land clearing continued,

delayed only by a stretch of grade that had to be thrown up. In 1878, a locomotive was purchased in San Francisco, along with several miles of iron track, made possible through issuance of bonds. It was further voted to have the rail cars built at Tumwater to spur the local economy.

The rail line was completed in July and the celebrated iron horse rolled in to a wild reception, opening up the hinterland to Olympia. Everyone who could find "gripping space" rode the train on its inaugural round trip, all in the area having had an invested interest in "their" railroad.

During the panic of 1873, the Northern Pacific made virtually no progress. Two years later, however, after rich finds of coal were discovered near the upper Puyallup River, about 25 miles east of Tacoma, new hopes gained impetus. Inasmuch as the road needed coal, both for its engines and to supply people along the route, an extension was planned. Fragments of the NP had been built in Minnesota, the Dakotas and Washington, but business had not developed as predicted on the Kalama-Tacoma link and the "city of destiny" had suffered from slow growth despite the efforts of the Tacoma Land Company. Finally, at great expense to himself, Charles B. Wright, of Philadelphia, president of the railroad had a shipment of iron rails brought around Cape Horn. The track bed was graded and rails laid. By 1877, a connection was completed to Wilkeson, and then to Carbonado. Coal rolled down the tracks to the port of Tacoma and on to Kalama for both domestic and export purposes. Until that time, only one train a day traveled the original link, but additional business soon spurred operations.

Tallest building west of the Mississippi was the boast of the Smith Tower, seen under construction above Alaska Steamship Co.'s Pier 2, about 1914. Only the steel frame of the then giant 42 story structure had been bolted together when this photo was taken. The pier at the center of the photo is historic Colman Dock with its landmark clock tower. The Smith Tower, today, dwarfed by other Seattle structures, was designed by Gaggin & Gaggin, and was hailed the world over on its completion. Oh, just in case anybody is interested, this photo was taken at precisely 3:33 p.m.; the Colman clock was seldom wrong.

As the seagull pictured the Lake Union Dry Dock Co. from the air in 1947, a host of government and commercial craft undergoing repairs. The yard has been a Seattle landmark for many decades.

By 1882, NP's tracks, by virtue of fresh funds and new incentive were fast moving west. On September 8, 1883, a gold spike was driven at Deer Lodge, Montana, completing the road's last link with its western terminus in Portland. The, NP fulfilled another dream by building a line across the Cascades. On June 6, 1887, direct communication was established by means of switchbacks, and the first train from the east puffed into Tacoma. The celebrated Stampede Pass Tunnel was completed in 1888, allowing the railroad to tap the vast resources of the territory. Other railroad companies then pulled political strings to gain right-of-way, and by the turn of the century, branches of railroads were creeping into nearly every productive whistlestop in Washington. Forests, mines and farms were now within reasonable distances of iron rails. More settlers were attracted west.

In 1893, the Great Northern Railroad, under the capable leadership of Jim Hill, king of the empire builders, came on strong. He had long visioned a Chicago to Seattle rail service connecting with a first-class transpacific service. He saw his dream come true in 1904-05 as powerful steam engines pulled freight and passenger cars across the pass to link up with the world's largest combination cargo-passenger liners — the steamships *Minnesota* and *Dakota,* homeporting at Seattle. These mammoth twins were each 622 feet in length, of 20,714 gross tons, and powered with 10,000 horsepower steam engines fed by several coal-fired boilers. James Hill esq. had put Seattle, the Queen City, on the map to stay, even though the embers of the Alaska gold rush had cooled down.

In 1909, the Chicago, Milwaukee, St. Paul and Pacific Railroad came west via Spokane, to both Tacoma and Seattle, and the previous year, the Spokane, Portland and Seattle Railroad began operations between Spokane and Portland. By this time, four transcontinental rail lines, including Union Pacific, either served Puget Sound directly or had major branch lines. Still the rivalry between Seattle and Tacoma continued.

One of the later major accomplishments was the completion of Great Northern's Cascade Mountain Tunnel, between Scenic and Berne, the longest railroad tunnel in the Americas, and one of the longest in the world. Chiseled through some eight miles of solid granite, with 34 miles of high-speed trackage, it replaced 43 miles of winding and precipitous mountain line. Tracklaying was commenced on Christmas Day in 1925 and completed in January 1929, at a then huge outlay of $25 million.

Though Seattle has grown much larger than Tacoma, both have become great commercial centers with prominent roles in world and domestic commerce. From the age of sail to the nuclear age it has been a thrilling and colorful march into the future.

One of the legends of our time. The story of the Foss Launch & Tug Company from a meagre little boathouse on the Tacoma waterfront to one of the nation's formidable tug and barge aggregations. It all started when Andrew and Thea Foss, seen at the top of the steps in the upper photo, began a boat rental service in the 1880's. Beginning with rowboats, they graduated to naptha launches, and then to gas, with the launch **COLUMBIA** in 1901. The fleet of tugs and launches is pictured as it began to grow after the turn of the century. The huge enterprise which maintained offices in both Seattle and Tacoma eventually replaced all of its old equipment with ultra modern tugs and barges of every description. A family operation until recent times, the firm has been taken over by the Dillingham Corp. interests.

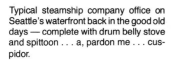

Typical steamship company office on Seattle's waterfront back in the good old days — complete with drum belly stove and spittoon . . . a, pardon me . . . cuspidor.

Father Time has a way of changing things. This is the Port of Olympia as it appeared (upper) in the late 1920's, and (below) as it looked just before the turn of the century. In the top picture, a host of ocean freighters load lumber at the port piers. Below, a party of three tugs, the **FRANCIE, BLUE STAR** and **SOPHIE** are seen. The sternwheelers are the **IRENE, CAPITAL CITY** and another, unidentified.

Contrasts in white and black. The immaculate four-masted bark **EDWARD SEWELL** comes into the old Seattle coal dock to take on a cargo of the black stuff. This "Downeaster," out of Bath, Maine, built in 1899, later became the **STAR OF SHETLAND** of the Alaska Packers fleet. Of 3,206 tons, the sizable square-rigger was finally broken up in Japan in 1935-36.

Chapter Eight
Maritime Miscellany

Nature knows no pause in progress
and development, and attaches her
curse to all inaction.
                    — Goethe

MANY GREAT MARITIME events have transpired in the history of Puget Sound in bygone years, but one that has had a big impact down through the decades was the establishment of the Puget Sound Naval Shipyard at Bremerton. Hidden among the narrow, deep channels of Kitsap County, about half way down the west shore of the Sound, Bremerton was to win out over its near neighbor Port Orchard as the site of the historic yard. To better understand Bremerton's role, we must first have a thumbnail sketch of Port Orchard. It is the seat of Kitsap County and one of the oldest settlements on Kitsap Peninsula. Tracing its beginnings back to 1854, William Renton and Daniel Howard landed near the towering forests rimming Port Orchard Bay (named by Captain Vancouver in honor of H. M. Orchard, of the ship *Discovery*). They built a sawmill and established a settlement complete with a shipyard, where in 1855, the citizens toasted their first ship to slide down the ways, a small 23 ton schooner, named *I. I. Stevens* for the territory's first governor. The village grew up around the mill and took on the name Sidney, after Sidney Stevens, who platted the townsite. The name was changed to Port Orchard in 1903.

The Port Orchard Naval Station post office was established in Sidney in the early 1890's. Port Orchard wrested the county seat away from Port Madison in a bitter campaign, and though it became keeper of the county records, Bremerton was destined to get the naval shipyard. It came after a long search by the government to find a secluded and deep waterway suitable for such an establishment. Bremerton got the nod, and to this day the yard has remained a vital factor in the nation's overall naval program, its facilities second to none. Numerous ships, the world's largest battlewagons of yesteryear and today's mightiest aircraft carriers and nuclear submarines have overhauled and repaired at the yard. And only a few miles away at Bangor, on Hood Canal, submarines are catered to. Bremerton is also the home of the USS *Missouri,* upon whose decks the surrender documents ending World War II were signed in Tokyo Bay. Now enshrined, thousands annually visit the "Mighty Mo" to recall that memorable date in history.

The city of Bremerton grew up around the navy yard. The establishment soon became the top industry in the economic life of Kitsap County, replacing many defunct lumber mills and commercial shipyards of an earlier era. The city later took over the communities of Charleston and Manette. William Bremer, a native of Germany who came west to Washington Territory in 1888 to engage in real estate investments platted the townsite in 1891. The settlement was named for him and it was he who played a leading role in attracting the shipyard by offering lands to the federal government at a cut rate. Bremer's offer was attractive to Uncle Sam, though the town, like so many other early Sound settlements had become a wild and wooly place where men of the cloth openly preached hellfire and brimstone sermons to bring the sinners to their knees.

Seattle fireboats **DUWAMISH,** foreground, and **ALKI** center, shoot graceful fountains of water, showing their firefighting potential. Astern is the Seattle Harbor Patrol boat. The **DUWAMISH** dating from 1909, was completely rebuilt at the now defunct Commercial Ship Repair yard on Bainbridge Island in late 1940's, making her one of the nation's most powerful firefighters. Many waterfront fires have been fought by the **ALKI** and **DUWAMISH.**

And certainly the need was evident, for the place was so unruly that Bremerton's first mayor, A. L. Croxton stated publicly:

"There were 17 saloons in Bremerton when I took office . . . the county was overrun by gamblers . . ."

Uncle Sam flexed his muscles before moving in, for with the aid of the Secretary of the Navy, pressure was brought to clear the streets of houses of iniquity and to give the town respectability.

East Bremerton, also known as Manette, sprang up in the 1890's around Bender's Mill, which was connected with the outskirts of Bremerton by a wooden trestle crossing a waterway. Initially, the site was named *Decatur,* after the vessel, but Manette is the name that has remained.

Bremerton became very official following establishment of the Puget Sound Naval Shipyard on September 16, 1891. To eliminate any commercial profiteering or loitering by the public near the yard gates, an ordinance was passed which made it a misdemeanor "to sell or roast peanuts, loaf, tell stories, whittle, spit or scatter litter near the establishment." Violators were subject to fines of from $5 to $25. The vendors and bums quickly dispersed, and except for those on official business the gate area was at times as quiet as a New England graveyard.

Somewhat ironical was the fact that the first ship to arrive at the shipyard for repairs was not an American naval craft, but the Japanese warship *Yamagucha*

Maru. She was followed in short order by the big battlewagon USS *Oregon,* which was to distinguish herself for a record run around Cape Horn during the Spanish American War.

The land originally purchased for the naval yard comprised 190 acres, but this was later expanded to 285 acres, and prior to World War II, the valuation of the buildings and improvements was some $65 million. Since then, it has climbed steadily. On occasion the cost of the modernization of a major aircraft carrier has exceeded the entire value of the yard. All types of naval ships can be accommodated. Several thousand civilians are employed in addition to Naval and Marine Corps personnel. Several ships, built from the keel up, have been completed at Bremerton, such as the 53,000 deadweight ton USS *Sacramento,* which at the time of her completion in 1963, was the largest and most powerful combination oiler, ammunition and supply ship ever built.

The No. 3 dock completed in 1919 is a shipbuilding facility, and before World War II was the largest of its kind in the world, with a length of 926 feet, a beam of 130 feet and a depth of 24 feet, holding some 21.8 million gallons of water. In 1935, a 825 foot long machine shop was erected at a cost of $1.3 million.

Today, massive commercial shipbuilding establishments in Japan and Europe, constructing supertankers up to a half million deadweight tons, have far surpassed in size the facilities at Bremerton. But from the military

Launching of the Seattle fireboat **DUWAMISH** at the Richmond Beach Shipbuilding Company in 1909. The 309 ton vessel cost $125,000 and was fitted with a 1,100 horsepower steam engine. She replaced the veteran fireboat **SNOQUALMIE.** Appearing more like a giant steel canoe than a fireboat, on becoming waterborne, she was an innovation in such craft, having been designed by McAllister & Bennett. The tug **GEORGE T.** is seen standing by.

Until the days of the completed Lake Washington Ship Canal, the old Stoneway Bridge ran across the west corner of Lake Union, complete with a double set of tracks. It was located near the present site of the old Fremont Bridge. The Fremont district is in the background.

South end of Lake Union when the old Southlake Inn and cafeteria were located there, along with some scattered houseboats and rafts of logs.

point of view the yard remains as a priority facility, having consistently boasted the best record of production and cost savings of any of America's counterpart government shipyards.

And speaking of naval events, probably no single event was met with more enthusiasm than the launching of the battleship *Nebraska,* at the Moran Brothers Shipyard in Seattle. Local folk were involved almost as much as when building their first railroad. The "people project" greatly increased employment at a crucial time. In 1900, Moran submitted a low bid for a first-class battleship, somewhat with tongue-in-cheek, as the maritime-oriented of the country appeared amused at a small Seattle yard trying to vie with the big-time eastern establishments for such a contract. The Moran yard had to its credit one small naval torpedo boat, the *Rowan,* turned out in 1897, and company boss, Robert Moran was confident his facility could tackle a battlewagon.

Congress had earlier appropriated a lump sum for the Navy to build four prime battleships in privately owned yards. Though Moran bid in at the lowest figure, it was still $182,000 higher than one fourth of the appropriation. The Navy secretary told the four low bidders that if they could bring their figures down to the government estimate they could share in the overall contract. Frantically Moran tried to get the figures down, despite the fact that the cost of building in the west was considerably greater than in the east. Going over the contract again and again with his estimators, it appeared virtually impossible to get the figure down without taking a financial loss. The Seattle Chamber of Commerce then got to work and agreed to cover by subsidy plan, $100,000 of the difference if Moran could come up with the rest. Several local citizens responded, but Moran said they

would have to cough up at least $120,000. The contract was finally signed with the Navy, one Seattle capitalist donating $5,000 outright.

Everybody that could cram into the shipyard was present when the *Nebraska* was launched on October 7, 1904. The keel had been laid on July 4, 1902 after a $750,000 expenditure was forthcoming for strengthening the ways and obtaining machinery and equipment. VIP's of both the states of Washington and Nebraska were present, the crowd so thick one could have walked across the yard on their heads. Bands blared forth amid flags, bunting and serpentine. Nebraska's Governor John Mickey presided, and it was his daughter Mary that broke the bottle of champagne across the ship's bow. All went off like clockwork as the 14,948 displacement ton, 435 foot battleship went down the ways. Robert Moran personally supervised every aspect of her construction. On the vessel's trial runs under pilot J. B. Libby, the *Nebraska* exceeded her contracted speed, plowing up Sound waters at a 19 knot sustained clip by virtue of her twin vertical triple expansion steam engines fed by 12 coal fired boilers, developing 21,283 horsepower.

When accepted by the Navy in 1907 after passing every test with flying colors, the vessel received acclaim far and wide. Carrying 49 officers and 857 enlisted men, the ship was armed with four 12 inch, eight 8 inch and twelve 6 inch guns plus several smaller pieces of armament. Sailing on into naval history, the *Nebraska* carried the "E" award for engine room excellence for many years.Though a major battlewagon in her day, the vessel would be dwarfed by the nuclear aircraft carriers of our time.

Another marine event that received national news coverage in the yesteryears, was the completion of the

Throughout the 1920's and 1930's Seattle's Lake Union served as a storage garage for idle or obsolete ships. This was a typical scene about 1929. The steel freighter **WEST HENSHAW** is at the center of the photo. Behind her is the big square-rigger **JAMES DOLLAR**, one of the largest commercial sailing vessels to fly the stars and stripes. An array of five and six-masted schooners and barkentines can be seen along the east shore of the lake.

Lake Washington Ship Canal and Hiram Chittenden (Ballard) Locks, in 1916. The fresh water lakes of Union and Washington were at last commercially connected with Puget Sound, fulfilling a dream that went back to the earliest settlers. Geologists claim that in the eons of time, evidences showed that some kind of a natural stream or river may have linked up the three bodies of water, and was in turn healed over by cataclysmic action. Be that as it may, the start by man to restore it as a canal for useful purposes was suggested soon after the settlers arrived. Few then could have guessed that the fulfillment of such a project would one day boast of a capacity on this continent second only to that of the Panama Canal. The monumental task of bringing the project to fruition was carried on from 1911-16, under the direction of Carl F. Gould. Ah, but we are getting ahead of ourselves, so let us go back to the beginning.

The initial action came in 1869, when a burly pioneer named H. L. Pike founded a little settlement in the wilderness near the portage of the two lakes, and named it Union City. He cleared the surrounding land and platted it out. Next he started digging something that resembled a crude irrigation ditch between the lakes to promote his suggestion of a future canal through which logs could be floated. He told his prosepctive investors that someday a canal might be built all the way to Puget Sound. Though some scoffed at such a wild suggestion, it eventually came to pass.

The impossible dream lay in limbo for two years, when Uncle Sam sent a delegation west to look over the lakes as a possible site for a naval shipyard, utilizing the fresh water for removal of sea growth from ships' bot-

toms. At that time, the expense of linking the lakes and digging a canal to salt-water appeared astronomical, and plans for a Lake Washington naval base were closeted. Again the dream appeared far over the horizon, but even as the Navy ruled out such possibilities, the local citizens kept the project alive in 1881, when the Washington Improvement Company was formed by Messrs. Denny, Bagley, McGilvra, and Smithers, with Thomas Burke acting as attorney and F. J. Whitworth as engineer. Their sole purpose was to construct the long elusive canal. Backed by a quarter million dollars, they began work on a waterway from Lake Washington and Lake Union, 16 feet wide with a drop of 12 feet. The contractor soon went bankrupt, and Bagley, Denny and Smithers assumed all of the firm's stock in 1886. They, in turn, changed the scope of the project to a canal with a six foot depth containing two locks. This would be sufficient to herd logs down from the timber-rich acreage around Lake Washington and back to the hinterland. The logging and lumber firms got behind the effort, and in 1887 a log flume was built. Before the undertaking was finished, funds ran short again and an appeal went out for federal assistance. Three years later, government surveyors once again came west to look over possibilities for an all-purpose canal.

Contingent on receiving the right-of-way from local government, favorable survey results prompted Congress to grant an initial grant of $25,000 to deepen Salmon Bay. That was in 1894, and a canal course was accordingly laid out from Ballard, west to Shilshole Bay and Puget Sound. Just as the government was beginning to get its feet solidly inside the door, some maladjusted individual, who was never apprehended, dynamited the gates of an existing small wooden locks and thwarted the movement of logs from the Lake Washington back lands. The ill-fated lock had been put into operation in 1899, under control of J. S. Brace who collected ten cents per thousand feet of all timber passing through. A proposal was made seven years later by James Moore to build a canal 60 feet wide and 25 feet deep with a single lock.

The government then got active again with an even more ambitious plan. Hiram Chittenden, district chief of the Army Engineers suggested a permanent masonry locks. Congress listened to both plans and finally granted funds permitting the blending of Moore's plan with that of the district chief, calling for a 75 foot wide canal with a 25 foot depth, utilizing a large and a small lock, side by side to be located in the Ballard area. In turn, the Lake Washington Canal Association was formed, and Chittenden was successful in getting the complete package approved by Congress. Work got underway in the early fall of 1911. Construction began at Ballard on the two locks, the larger with extreme masonry walls, 1,425 feet in length and the smaller, 690 feet. Chamber widths were 80 and 30 feet respectively,

both with lifts of from six to 26 feet. Lake Washington was lowered artificially from 29.8 feet above sea level on Puget Sound to 21 feet. The Montlake Cut was also dredged out.

The small lock was opened to traffic on July 30, 1916 and the large lock four days later. A city-wide celebration to commemorate the completion of the overall project was held on July 4, 1917, as the SS *Roosevelt,* formerly Admiral Peary's Arctic exploration ship, and the U.S. Engineers sternwheel snag puller *Swinomish,* led a large marine parade witnessed by thousands of onlookers lining the canal banks for its entire eight mile length. Especially was the crowd thick at the locks to witness the mechanical wonder as the big facility lowered or raised a ship in only eight minutes and smaller lock in only four. Open 24 hours a day, the locks grew in popularity, and by 1940 was catering to three million tons of freight and over one million passengers per annum.

A long elusive dream had been fulfilled. The first vessel with a payload to pass through the canal waterway and locks was the Black Ball steamer *Sioux,* bursting to the gunwhales with delighted passengers. Since 1916-17, thousands of vessels of every description have trans-

Nostalgic scene on Lake Union, taken May 13, 1929. The little ferry **MOUNT VERNON** is seen, center, outbound for Puget Sound. In the foreground is the old steam tug **SEA MILL,** while at the dock is the SS **INTERNATIONAL,** of the International Packing Company. She was built at Ashtabula, Ohio in 1919. Capitol Hill is in the background.

Historic day — the opening of the Montlake Cut showing the waters of Lake Washington sweeping into the newly created channel leading to Lake Union. Lake Washington had to be lowered several feet when the cut was opened. Later, the Montlake Bridge was erected. The waterway today rims the sprawling University of Washington and the Husky football stadium, one of the few places anywhere where both vehicles and vessels bring fans to the games. In 1885, there was only a ditch between the lakes.

ited the canal, but the large proportion of commercial vessels down through the years have been greatly exceeded by growing numbers of pleasure craft.

How the Puget Sound country was changed from a virgin paradise to an industrial giant in a century and a quarter is as amazing as the metamorphosis process of the caterpillar into a butterfly, but, not necessarily in that order, for nature lovers may look upon the change as just the reverse. Though Puget Sound is still endowed with much natural beauty, the metropolitan sprawl is well underway, and the day may come when the cities of Bellingham, Everett, Seattle, Tacoma and Olympia will blend into one solid metropolis rimming the eastern and southern shores of Puget Sound. The air has been sullied by the emission from pulp, steel, and lumber mills, as well as from countless other types of factories. A vast network of freeways with a never ending flow of traffic snake in and out of Seattle and Tacoma while super airliners fly the skies from Sea-Tac International and Boeing fields. Freight trains roll in with longer and longer chains of box, flat and tank cars, while stinky diesel trucks and buses roar down the grey ribbons.

Containerliners, bulkers and tankers utilizing Puget Sound waterways grow ever larger, and superferries, tugboats, fishboats, pleasure craft and naval vessels are everywhere. Forests have been leveled clear back and beyond the foothills as suburbanitis spreads and spreads and spreads.

Yes, indeed, the scene has completely changed, and this writer must agree that it is not all for the best, even though the existing drama masquerades as progress. It is little wonder that people still talk of the good old days. Though we have never had life easier than today, still much color, adventure and natural beauty has passed from the scene. Those in the crowded communities speed out of town constantly to the more pastoral haunts in the San Juan Islands and along the western shores of Puget Sound where progress in many areas has been at a snail's pace and hopefully will remain that way. One can't dwell on it, lest he be labeled senile, but sometimes a glimpse into the past can be as refreshing as a cool glass of water on a hot summer day.

Those pioneers of old had plenty of grit and determination, but few could have visualized in their wildest

This is the way the Montlake Cut appeared after completion, as a parade of vessels pass through. These pictures were taken before the erection of the Montlake Bridge.

dreams the Puget Sound of today. New frontiers are fast becoming a thing of the past, and man must now fight to keep from destroying his environment, over-population and pollution being already at the door.

The arrival of Captain Vancouver; the rebellion of the Indian and the determination of the white settler are but faded chapters of time and eternity. Though man and his ways constantly change, the Almighty never changes, nor do his great landmarks which man cannot move. No wonder they called Mount Rainier, "the mountain that was God." It has watched over the entire transition of Puget Sound and has not changed one iota. Perhaps at the end of this age, after man has brought himself to ruin, will this great mountain of eternal snows again blow its top and send rivers of fiery lava down its slopes to cover the traces.

THE END

July 4, 1917, the government fisheries streamer **ROOSEVELT,** formerly Admiral Peary's Arctic exploration ship (later a tug) leads the marine parade through the newly opened Lake Washington Ship Canal which connected LAKE Washington and Lake Union with Shilshole Bay and Puget Sound. In the lower photo, the Fremont Bridge opens its mouth wide to let the vessels pass through into Lake Union. Behind the Fremont Bridge is the now non-existent Stoneway trestle. Note the crowds lining the shores.

Like a Mutt and Jeff, the contrast between these two automobile ferries, is, as one would say in the modern vernacular, "far out." The **ACORN,** above, built in 1924, along with a similar ferry, the **DECEPTION PASS,** were designed for the Oak Harbor (Whidbey Island) — Utsaladdy (Camano Island) service, operated by Berte Olson, who later earned the title of "the Tugboat Annie of Hood Canal") by virtue of a later ferryboat service on that waterway. She was a full-fledged skipper, and was active up till 1950. The **ACORN** would have been dwarfed by the mighty superferry **SPOKANE** of the 1970's, almost seven times longer than the 65 foot **ACORN.** The 20 knot **SPOKANE** and her sister ferries, breeze across from Seattle to Winslow and to Bremerton as well as other ports, under the banner of the Washington State Ferry System.

Honk! Honk! Let's get that traffic moving! Typical scene on the old Fremont Bridge just after the bridge had been raised to let a ship pass through. There was no Aurora Bridge in those days and most of the traffic used the Fremont Bridge to get across the canal. Note the old Seattle trolley cars. Bryant Lumber mill is seen, its tall stack being rebuilt.

Upper photo — Locomobile Pathfinder does a little publicity work for the AAA in getting new and better roads for Washington State to list in the Automobile Blue Book, back in the good old days. The four enterprising gentlemen are evidently taking their work seriously. Lower photo — Making a big splash on the streets of downtown Seattle, the dapper gent poses in his spanking new horseless carriage.

166

Built by famous Seattle shipbuilder Robert Moran, at his luxury hideaway at Rosario on Orcas Island in 1917, was the three-mast schooner-yacht **SANWAN**. She was the last vessel he built and was for his own pleasure. The 219 ton craft is seen in upper photo passing through the Montlake Cut in Seattle. In the lower photo, she is shown sliding down the ways in 1917. The vessel ended up several years later as a California scientific vessel, many of her lavish appointments going by the wayside.

A handsome fighting ship in every respect, no ship in Uncle Sam's Navy had a more avid group of followers, for many Seattleites assisted the yard financially in landing the contract for the **NEBRASKA.**

A bow-on view of the new battleship **NEBRASKA** at the Moran yard about 1904 or 1905. Note the beautiful scrollwork and bow emblem, tantamount to a figurehead and trailboards. Her semi-rounded pilot house and flying bridge gave navigators an overall view.

The famous Moran Brothers Shipyard in Seattle, which built the city's one and only battleship, the **NEBRASKA,** in the early years of this century. The 14,000 ton dreadnaught is seen at the yard, (center right), amid a host of steam schooners, a passenger steamer and a government vessel. The Moran yard began operating in the late 1890's, and latched on to much of the bonanza during the Alaska gold rush activity.

Port Blakely Harbor during the World War I years was still a busy place. The two sailing vessels at the right are the **BENJ. F. PACKARD** and the **J. D. PETERS.** The little cannery tender repairing on the shore is the **MORZHOVOI** built at Seattle in 1917.

The modernized Port Blakely Mill as it appeared during the World War I era before it began its steep decline. Notice the New England style officials' homes built in the earlier days of the bustling lumber port. The steamer **MONTICELLO**, beneath the bow of the four-mast bark, in lower photo, operated for many years between Seattle and Port Blakely.

PORT BLAKLEY MILLS
MARCH. 26-1918
Pt. BLAKLEY. WASH.

Two chicks and a super sedan visit the Puget Sound Naval Shipyard in the late 1920's. The big fighting ship in the background is in for repairs. A few curious sailors appear to be discussing the girls rather than the car.

From the Seattle Harbor Patrol dock when the fleet was in, Navy gigs, and other small craft would transport sailors back and forth from the big battlewagons, cruisers, destroyers and auxiliary craft.

The late Joshua Green, pioneer Puget Sound steamboater and banker, receives honorary lifetime membership to the Puget Sound Maritime Historical Society. Mr. Green, left, died in 1975 at the age of 105. Center is society president Ralph Hitchcock, and the late Jim Valentine, blowing old steamer whistle, an ex-society president who was lost in a boating tragedy off the Columbia River bar in the 1960's.

Proudly posing for his picture, "Chief Warren" was a mainstay for most of the big parades in Puget Sound cities for many years.

Scuttlebutt Pete whose real name was Stewart Osborn, was a long time column writer for Pacific Motor Boat Magazine. Crippled by advance arthritis he kept close tabs on all the boating activities on Puget Sound and had friends throughout the maritime world. The "Piling Busters," a group of towboaters presented him with a marine radio telephone which kept him in close contact with the towboaters who had a big role in his column. Mr. Osborn passed away in 1955.

One of Seattle's celebrated citizens of yesteryear was financier C. A. Kinnear, a descendent of pioneer stock. Here he puts on his special driver's gloves for a ride to his place of business.

The yachting scene has changed in our age, but this is what the West Seattle Yacht Club looked like back when. Pretty fancy clubhouse.

Another view of the West Seattle Yacht Club with the Seattle waterfront in the background across Elliott Bay. Rail tracks rimmed the bay shores.

On August 11, 1901, this was the scene at the West Seattle landing after the little sidewheel ferry **CITY OF SEATTLE**, paddled over from the central Seattle waterfront. By the way they are pouring off the vessel, it must have been a profitable run. The **CITY OF SEATTLE** was the city's first salt-water ferry, built at Portland in 1888. She ended her days in California waters.

An overall view of the West Seattle ferry dock and the West Seattle Yacht Club. The ferry **WEST SEATTLE** is seen in her slip, a steam sidewheeler, built by the Heath Yard in Tacoma in 1907, for the West Seattle Land & Improvement Company. Note the sign advertising good view lots for an easy down payment. To the right of the ferry slip is the West Seattle Yacht Club and to the right of the clubhouse, the flour mill and dock. In the background is the West Waterway into which flowed the Duwamish River. A rare collection of pleasure craft dot the bay waters.

A strange combination — a fleet of idle vessels tied up off Duwamish Head, with the whirligigs of Luna Park beyond their bowsprits. The vessels, from left, are the schooners **ALICE, JOSEPH RUSS,** the power vessel **F.H. FOLSOM** and the small schooner **ALVA.**

Speed gets· 'em! The latest in speed boats, the **SEA COLT,** struts her stuff on Lake Washington in greener years. Most had to settle for canoes or skiffs.

Talk about luxury. This is strictly for the man who has everything. Note that fancy wicker furniture on the afterdeck of the luxury cruiser **LAURELHURST**. This picture was taken on Lake Washington, but we have been unable to identify the prominent looking gentlemen posing for the camera.

Harbor Island, in the background, is Seattle's man-made industrial Island seen here just after its completion. The island actually traces its origin back before the turn of the century when sailing vessels used it as a ballast dumping grounds.

Aerial view of Harbor Island in the 1930's, looking northward toward metropolitan Seattle.

Under construction, Seattle's Smith Tower (L. C. Smith), tallest building west of the Mississippi at the time of construction (1914).

Pioneer Square in old Seattle before its traditional totem pole and covered waiting station were in place. Note horses and buggies and trolley street cars. Same buildings, restored, still stand today.

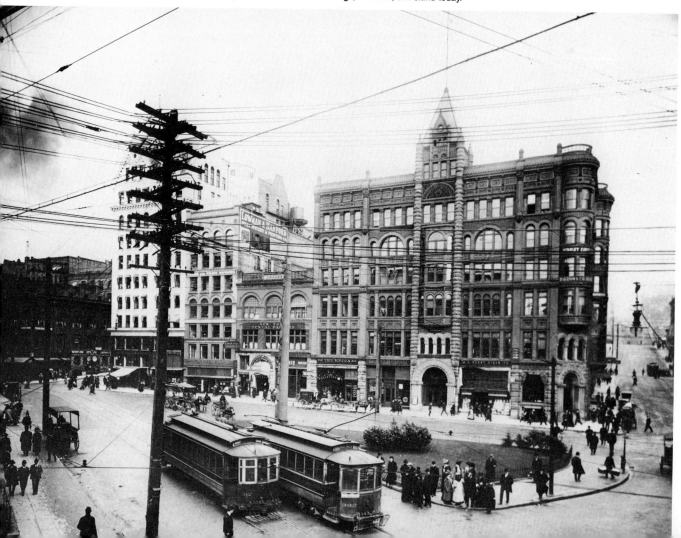

Anderson steamer **URANIA** at Juanita Dock on Lake Washington in the year 1907. Courtesy Captain Bob Matson.

Long before the days of the super ferryboats, passengers and freight went to and from Bremerton by steamers such as are seen at the local dock. This picture probably was taken about the turn of the century.

This is believed to be an early shot of Madison Park on Lake Washington, with the steamers **XANTHUS,** and the **URANIA** both with good passenger loads. Note the gazebo type boathouse at left.

The Yesler Street Landing on Lake Washington in bygone days shows at left, the steamer **L. T. HAAS** and the **XANTHUS.** The **HAAS,** operated with the **WILDWOOD** for Interlaken Steamship Company. Courtesy Capt. Bob Matson.

And that's the way it was, if one wanted to take his vehicle aboard the ferryboat at Port Townsend in 1937. It was raining hard, the line was long and tempers short. By contrast, in 1975, the state ferry **OLYMPIC** leaves Townsend for Keystone on Whidbey Island.

The before and after — Fortuna Park dock as it appeared in 1938 and again in 1975. Top photo courtesy Capt. Bob Matson, the lower, as Joe saw the same place in 1975.

Scene of the old Lake Washington Shipyards at Houghton as the area appeared in 1975. Veteran craft at dockside is the retired State ferry **KEHLOKEN.**

Kirkland waterfront in 1975 has vastly changed since the days of the old Kirkland ferry dock.

Would you believe it? This is Bellevue landing on Meydenbauer Bay as of May 30, 1914. Well, that is just what it is, and the ferry at the slip is the steam propelled **LESCHI.** Business doesn't appear to be good, with a single car, a horse and buggy and few passengers standing about. In those years, Bellevue was a tiny pastoral village, with a few stores and surrounding farms. Who would have guessed that by the 1970's it would become the fourth largest city in the state.

Peaceful Meydenbauer Bay as of 1975. This was once the locale of the Bellevue Ferry Dock and the moorage for the whaling fleet. Today its shores are marked with apartments and yacht moorages.

Once the site of the old Madison Park ferry dock on Lake Washington, the same scene in 1975 had changed considerably. In this general area, the city has seen many changes through the years.

Leschi Park in 1975, scene of a boat basin and recreational area. This was once the headquarters of the Anderson Steamboat Co., and boathouse where much of the activity on Lake Washington was centered.

Ex-Medina Ferry dock in 1975. The building was the old waiting room for the steamer passengers in bygone decades. It now serves, among other things, as the Medina City Hall, in a plush Lake Washington residential district.

The East Seattle Ferry landing on Mercer Island is but a memory. Now a fine residential area, Lake Washington passenger craft once made frequent calls here.

Roanoke on Mercer Island as it appeared in 1938 in a photo by Capt. Bob Matson, and again as "Joe" photographed it in 1975 — a portal without a ferry dock.

Veteran Puget Sound tug **MAGIC** rests at dockside in Seattle. She served for many years as a unit of the Admiralty Tug Boat Co., a subsidiary of Puget Sound Tug Boat Co. The old hulk in the background is the **WILLIAM H. SMITH**, built as a full-rigged ship at Bath in 1883, seen here converted to one of the Sound's first floating canneries as was the more famous **GLORY OF THE SEAS.** The vehicle on the dock speaks for itself.

Seattle waterfront in the 1920's, showing Pier D, leased by the Nelson Steamship Company. The line was a victim of the depression years. Nelson, headquartered in San Francisco, once operated more than 30 steel steam schooners and sailing vessels, mostly coastwise and intercoastal. Note the vintage cars on the pier.

Activity on the Mukilteo waterfront. The SS **TREMONT,** one of the largest vessels under the American flag when built in 1902, was a 490 foot, 9,600 gross ton ship seen here taking on lumber for foreign ports. In the foreground is the launch **NORENE.** A trading post was established at Mukilteo as early as 1860. An Indian peace treaty was also signed there (1855).

The proud liner **ORIZABA,** stands out at the repair yard, believed to be the old Moran establishment. The liner was built in 1889 for the Ward Line service on the Atlantic seaboard. She came out west and in 1906 became a unit of the Northwestern Steamship Co. Later she joined the Alaska Steamship Co. fleet. The 327 foot long vessel operated as the Alaska passenger ship **NORTHWESTERN** for many years, her demise coming at Dutch Harbor on June 4, 1942, while serving as a floating dormitory. The Japanese put an aerial bomb down her funnel and claimed they had bagged a first-class naval vessel. In photo, foreground, the dredge **PORTLAND** and **PUGET NO. 6.** To the stern of the **ORIZABA,** is the bow section of the famous gold ship SS **PORTLAND.** Centennial Mill Co. is at upper left. The naval vessel in the background is probably the **NEBRASKA.** Photo taken about 1905.

Two docks that have weathered the storm of time and progress, are the old Ainsworth Dunn Dock (Pier 14) and (Pier 15) the Union oil dock along the Seattle waterfront. Known today as Piers 70 and 71, the former has become a tourist attraction, with shops, restaurants and other attractions, but the latter is still used by Union Oil Co. In this photo, probably taken about 1930, two British flag Blue Funnel freighters are at dockside, the **PROTESILAUS** and **TYNDAREUS,** among the largest cargo carriers then operating in the Pacific. A small Union Oil coastal tanker is at the Union dock. Note how the rails and roads are still on trestles and piling prior to the filling in and erection of Alaskan Way, once known as Railroad Avenue.

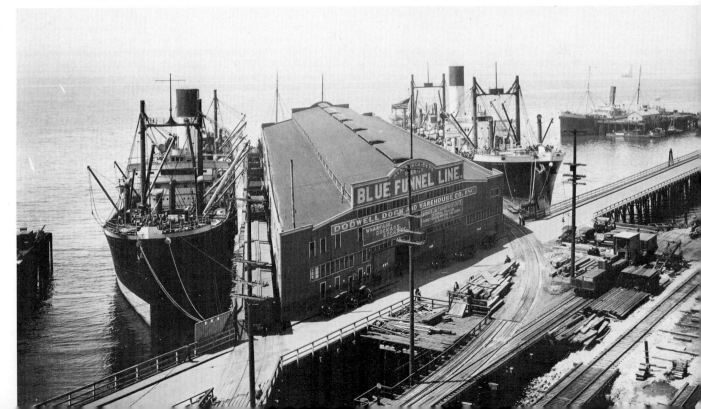

A view of the Houghton steamer landing of yesteryear, with Hunts Point in the background. Courtesy Capt. Bob Matson.

Loading lumber at an Elliott Bay pier, is seen the four-mast schooner **ARIEL**. The 726 ton vessel, built by M. Turner at Benicia, Calif. in 1900, was lost at Inuboyesaki, Japan in 1917. Directly astern of the schooner is Queen Anne Hill, the high school at its crest.

Three lumber schooners moored in peaceful water in the harbor at Everett, one of which has a cargo of piling.

The long time Seattle tug **ROOSEVELT**, of Washington Tug & Barge Co., is seen here as she appeared when serving as Admiral Peary's flagship on his expedition to the North Pole. At that time, she was rigged as a three-masted auxiliary power schooner. Admiral Robert Peary succeeded in reaching the North Pole April 6, 1909. The famed Arctic explorer died in 1920.

Head room only at the J. F. Duthie & Company shipyard in Seattle
for the launching of a big steel freighter during World War I.